Towards Peace

in

Jammu, Kashmir
&
Ladakh

Map Not to Scale

Towards Peace
in
Jammu, Kashmir
&
Ladakh

Dr. Majid Siraj

Manas Publications
New Delhi-110 002 (INDIA)

Manas Publications

(Publishers, Distributors, Importers & Exporters)
4858, Prahlad Street,
24, Ansari Road, Darya Ganj,
New Delhi - 110 002 (INDIA)

Ph.: (O) 23260783, 23265523, (R) 27131660
Fax: 011 - 23272766
E-mail: manaspublications@vsnl.com

© Majid Siraj

First Published: 2003

ISBN 81-7049-162-2

Typeset at
Manas Publications

Printed in India at
Shri Bala Ji Art Press, Delhi
and Published by Mrs Suman Lata for
Manas Publications, 4858, Prahlad Street,
24, Ansari Road, Darya Ganj,
New Delhi - 110 002 (INDIA)

Preface

Historically, the Treaty of Westphalia for peace (1648) between sovereign nations, the Vienna Congress, Versailles and United Nations resolution on Kashmir all forged multilateral agreements to save succeeding generations from the scourge of war. Limitations on war were emphasised by philosophers like Hugo Grotius (1625) who hoped to promote peace, laying out the foundations of tolerance towards religious doctrines. All United Nations did for Kashmir from 1948, is to effect a ceasefire culminating in a negative peace. Resolutions were passed, only foreboding another war in the future. The dispute remained unresolved. Fourth war between India and Pakistan is imminent and this time it may end up in a major human disaster. UN has not acted with foresight and used Article 2 of its charter to put into practice effective and collective measures for prevention and removal of threat to peace. Boutros Ghali, ex- Secretary General, explained that the failure of UN to settle the dispute was because article 6 of the charter and not 7 was used in the conduct of the case, the so- called six and a half factor. Peace was forestalled by expediency of major powers who responded tangentially to this crisis due to manifest lack of interest in the region and preoccupation with conflicts elsewhere in the world. In post cold war era, 'self determination' uprisings are discouraged as a policy of NATO's security strategy.

All major faiths have advocated making peace and in our assumptions we consider there is consent for peace in Kashmir from all sections of epistemic societies. There are mammoth challenges of even making a start in the peace process. The first obstacle to overcome, is public stereotyped hostile imagery and then to establish an amicable equanimity between the politicians of all parties. Rhetoric for peace is flying to and fro while guns are blazing in the mountains of Kashmir. It is intended to facilitate an unbiased understanding of issues based on theoretical analysis and empirical research done in other conflict areas and use them to focus on the possibilities and advantages of peace. Selection of paradigms offered may prove useful in the pre-negotiating phase as thought breaking models and create a political atmosphere conducive to movement across the table. This approach may obviate impediments and explore new ideas not considered so far. The emphasis has been to serve the crucial needs of the protagonists towards a triumphant march for reason, in the hope that they can sell these paradigmatic ideas to their people. In the conduct of peace making soul searching needs to be done without using a mandate blinders approach.

The Kashmir dispute has some built-in positive features like commonalties of culture and language shared by the whole subcontinent and strong elements of homogeneity. Indian Prime Minister Mr Vajpayee after his bus ride to Pakistan told reporters, "We discussed at length and did not need an interpreter" is a notable signal. All communities are aware that they have to live together notwithstanding the conflict ridden nationalist diatribe exchanged by some politicians. A brief insight into the history of conflict which started in 1947 is given. This became the antithesis in the political life of the state. British relinquished their supremacy over Kashmir as a part of the process of decolonizing the subcontinent. India and Pakistan were created as two dominions carved out of the empire. Their assets and liabilities were divided just like a family settlement. All the attention now focused on who gets Kashmir?

The wars fought in Kashmir, Clauswitzean by nature, contravened criterion of Jus ad bellum. There was no clear winner, both sides could not justify the death and destruction caused and it was unclear who was more at fault if you applied the concept of comparative justice. It is the hard talk of realist thinking impelling them to determine a result by military means which has to be feared the most. Citizens of all fractured parts of Kashmir are trying to reckon how the state regulates their lives, faced with challenges of seeking to find out where it is in their society' their identity is located ? These factors have ebbed on an unbroken revolution, rooted in unrest from political injustices and to some extent structural transformations. Rapid turn-over of daily events in the region has entrenched a belief that people are mere gambits in power politics.

Order and peace could be established if people were treated with respect. 'Disorder' it is believed is a result of excessive authority. (Peter Kropotkin 1842-1921) The erstwhile National Conference rule was perceived to be authoritarian in the face of countervailing political factions. However if Kropotkin's aphorism stands scrutiny in the neo-realist lobby, the new regime in Jammu & Kashmir have a chance to prove its worthiness. The Common Minimal Program' (CMP) propounded by the ruling People's Democratic Party (PDP) (see Appendix 1) and its National Congress consociational partner has bold measures stipulated to lower the scale of authority.) The CPM promise of repealing POTA (Prevention of Terrorism Act) and disbanding the infamous State Task Force is already having an impact on the lives of the people, who thronged the streets celebrating Eid with signs of relief written all over their faces.

Dr. Majid Siraj

Contents

Preface   5

PART I
Foundations of Kashmir Dispute

Introduction   17
Chapter 1   Historical Perspective: An Appraisal   19
Chapter 2   Genesis of Conflict: British Legacy   23

PART II
Conflict Resolution

Introduction   29
Chapter 3   Correlates of Peace : Philosophical Inquiry   31
Chapter 4   Domestic Front   37
Chapter 5   International Community and Kashmir   43
Chapter 6   Limitations   53

PART III
Dialectics Of Kashmir Dispute

Introduction   57
Chapter 7   Impact of Conflict on People of Kashmir   59
Chapter 8   Human Rights Fifty Years On   65

Chapter 9   Nuclear Arms / Terrorism & Kashmir   73
Chapter 10   Dialectical Analysis / True Cost   83

PART IV
Revisiting Conflict : Suggested Solutions

Introduction   93
Chapter 11   Notes on Paradigms : Antecedent Factors   97
Chapter 12   Paradigms   113
Chapter 13   Status in quo   123
Chapter 14   Conjoint Rule   129
Chapter 15   Partial Autonomy.   147
Chapter 16   Independence : Modified Dixon Plan   151
Chapter 17   Comparative Peace Process: Trusteeship   161
Chapter 18   Rebuilding Kashmir: Peace Keeping.   175

Conclusion & Epilogue   179
Post Script :   Organisation for South Asian Peace (Proposals)

Appendix   191
Index   197

1930-British Residency in Kashmir (known to be the most beautiful in all of British Empire.) This is where real power resided and could have been determinant of the future of Kashmir.

Floating gardens of Kashmir harvested exotic vegetables illustrated here during Mughal times. Striking amongst all were the lotus roots (Nadroo) shown being extracted by boatmen (Hanji). Names of vegetables as used now are also given in Urea.

Khandhar Kashmir

A B D A L I

S   I   K   H   S

Attak

J A T S Lahore

Delhi

Agra *A V A D H*

Luckhnow

Allahabad Bhutan

Ajmer Banaras Patna

Ahmedabad *B E N G A L*

Surat Calcutta

M A H A R A T A S B I H A R

Bombay Nagpur

Poona *N I Z A M*

Goa Hyderabad

T I P U

Kalikat Madras

Pondicharry

Cochin

Map Not to Scale

Afghan rule in Kashmir (1752-1818) Ahmad Shah Abdali ruled Kashmir
with mindless ferocity. His empire shown here, extended into Kashmir,
Punjab and beyond, in the backdrop of a subcontinent fragmented in
monarchial absolutism.

Part I

Foundations of Kashmir Dispute

 **Introduction:**

As we approach the problem today, it appears like an asymmetric war between state and people on the one hand and an interstate conflict between two powerful nations on the other. There is evidence of an uprising from disaffected masses who challenge legitimacy and order in carte blanche authority of the regime who governs over them. Insurgents perceive themselves as instrument of change. As political analysts we can only make observations on the basis of a study of the empirical knowledge of events as seen on a daily basis and chronicled in the archives. The factual feedback on events of the pro-active politics is fortunately still within reach of human memory. Most nations of the world including the USA or France came upon one revolution and achieved nationhood. Not so in Kashmir. For many hundreds of years they were subjects of a repressive oligarchial rule and their revolts against injustices were muzzled with wanton force. That background has a bearing on the causal relation of the events of today.

In the last big political change in the subcontinent of the partition in 1947, Kashmir was also partitioned but not on the basis of ethnic divide as in India nor as an amicable settlement between the two dominions but as a result of machination and an open fight between the two nascent states. The tug tore the state of Jammu and Kashmir apart and wrecked prospects of peace for the future of its people. An insight is given into the role British played at the time of inception of troubles in Kashmir. How and why the former masters gradually abandoned their responsibilities? Preoccupations in cold war politics and factors leading up to determinism in the politics of Kashmir resulted in waning interest by international community and in escalation of the conflict. The two chapters that follow are an attempt to abridge the milestones of the recent travails in the political history of Kashmir in keeping with the truism as revealed to us by the historians. We must not loose sight of the fact that truth is a social construct rooted in knowledge deeply enmeshed in power from countervailing forces of occupation after occupation and subjugation of the voices expressed. It follows implicitly that this composit peaceful society remains divided and its population dissipated.

Historical perspective of Kashmir is replete with successive invasions, resulting in imperious violent rule coming from its neighbouring and far away countries interminably over many centuries. It will become manifest why there is lack of respect shown for the people by the colonisers ? Why was it that they were treated as serfs ? Occupation regimes were presiding over rapidly proselytising community, constantly stifling their Eros and pride and presaging a rebellious civilisation.

Historical Perspective:
An Appraisal

In 1931 a political revolt was heralded for the first time in history against the ruling Maharaja. British had a resident in Kashmir during this period. He was in Kashmir to keep the supremacy over the sovereignty of Maharaja extant. British played a moderating role to alleviate the suffering of the people and set up measures like the Glancy commission to investigate injustices of the totalitarian regime. The suffering was replete with blatant atrocities inflicted on otherwise demure and fabian people. Their travails through a turbulent history deserve a mention in depth. In 1847 it was Britain who gifted Kashmir to a local despicable warlord, Gulab Singh, and transferred the political control of governance to him. Gulab Singh earned the name, the Himalayan Fox, for his duplicitous activities against his employers, the Sikh rulers in Punjab (Herbert Edwards 1872 London). He collaborated with British to defeat the Sikhs and cut off food supplies to the Sikh army to help the British. Realising the traitorous role played by him the Sikh ruler Rani Jindan stripped the fox of his control of Jammu and offered the whole of the state of Jammu & Kashmir to the British as 'War indemnity'. Kashmir state was completely in the hands of the British and ruled from India. This could have been a turning point in the history of Kashmir, as will be discussed later on.

Gulab Singh, realising his predicament, helped British in providing strategic assistance in transit of forces through Khyber pass to invade Afghanistan and at the same time as trying to invade Tibet which in effect would have cut off trade and supplies to India. The incumbent Governor General Sir Henry Hardinge (1844) realising the duplicity, wrote to Queen Victoria that Gulab must be rewarded for his collaboration even though he is the "Rascal of Asia" and Kashmir state be transferred to him, because the war indemnity could not be recovered from the Sikhs. They had no money (their treasure was stolen by Gulab). Gulab was willing to part with that money so desperately needed by Indian treasury. After the Sikh war II, on March 9 was 1846, the Sikh ruler Dilip Singh signed and ratified Peace treaty with British. As reparation Jammu and Kashmir was ceded to East India Company. Just a week later, this Himalayan paradise was sold to villain Gulab Singh, for a trivial sum of Rs 7,500,000 (£107,140) and Treaty of Amritsar was signed on the 16th March, 1846. Gulab paid money he had earlier plundered from his former masters, the Sikhs. Britain not only wanted the money but also saw benefit in making Gulab as ruler of Kashmir and buttress a first line of defence against Afghans. Hardinge said that Sutlej and Kashmir border was 300 miles of ungentle mountains and to maintain an army with no support for six months of the year was infeasible. Gulab paid Rs. 2.5 Millian less than 10 Million the Sikhs were having to pay, because British kept the Kulu valley and Mandi across river Beaas.

In reliance on Article 9 of the Treaty, the British would still protect Kashmir from invasions. Pursuant to Article 10, the ruler of Kashmir would accept the British Supremacy and in token of obedience give every year one horse, 12 Ibex goats and cashmere shawls. He could not exchange or trade off any territory without the concurrence of the British (Article 6). Subordinate to this covenant in the Treaty the Ruler could not have signed accession of the state to India in 1947, without prior approval from the British. Was there a covert decree?

The British masters now expected Gulab and Sikhs together to be the first line of defence and repulse Afghans and Muslims from Central Asia in the event of their incursions. Gulab having bought Kashmir now marched in to claim his acquisition. He was repulsed by Shiekh Imam, the Sikh governor in office at the time. Imam had consolidated power with help from the local tribes. Gulab turned to British for help. Hardinge obliged and 12 field guns and 8 regiments of infantry finally sealed the fate of Kashmiris into the clutches of a fiendish monarchical rule, requited a century later on 27th October. 1947 as part of a process in bringing a logical end to the imperium. Armies from Pakistan and India, still controlled by British officers, fought as enemies in an open war. The most crucial political artefacts in the history of Kashmir, were the maps drawn by two important people. It was James Abbot, a British officer who demarcated boundaries of Kashmir in August 1847 and one hundred years later it was another British officer, Cyril Radcliffe, who was demarcating these boundaries. It was at the behest of Mountbatten that Radcliffe made a deliberate error in allocating Gurdaspor and Zira districts to India to enable land access to Kashmir (Lamb). These lines have become the snares for the necks of millions of people.

Genesis of Conflict:

British Legacy

An inquiry is warranted into the role of underlying factors for what Edward Azar termed as the Protracted Social Conflict (PSC) in societies like that of the dominions of South Asia, extended into the essence of conflict in Kashmir. Kashmir is uniquely placed in the political collage of South Asia with a widespread communal content. It has been engaged in its struggle expressed as a search for identity and security needs. It is contiguous with three civilisations of Central Asia, Tibeto-Chinese and South-Asian which have rooted into the fabric of the society. In the backdrop of this diverse ethnopolitical landscape, the geo-political lines of control divide the state into three regions administered in large part by India, north-western region by Pakistan and a strip of steppes ridges bordering Tibet, by China.

The conceptual understanding of events which followed, posits a complexity of the anarchical system pervading in the immediate post-colonial period of the region. The war started when Pathans from Pakistan stormed in to restrain Maharaja from inflicting atrocitis on Muslims in Jammu and the Indian army was flown in immediately to drive the Pathans out. Indian Prime Minister Mr Nehru, himself a Kashmiri, justified marshalling every available Indian soldier into Kashmir as a messianic vocation. Pakistan army engaged itself in the ensuing battle to stop the advancing Indian army. All out war ensued within the confines of the state. Sir Frank Messervy, the Commander-in-Chief, stated that he was surprised to find Mountbatten directing military operations in Kashmir on a daily basis. The mantle of Governor General fell from him (Peace Committee 1953). One could critique the appointment of Lord Mountbatten as the executive responsible to perform the last rites in the dissolution of the colony. (Siraj)

Partition was the most violent event in the recorded history of India. The legacy left indelible marks of violence and simmering flames in Kashmir. Kashmir in 1947 fall was not a putative Westphalian state, because the erstwhile ruler was under the supremacy of the British. As an outcome of decolonizing process of the subcontinent, Britain relinquished their supremacy over Kashmir. It was assumed that by a deed of declared intent, Lord Mountbatten and Mr Nehru entered into a social contract with people of Kashmir through their leader Shiekh Mohomed Abdulla and the Ruler, and offered them a kind of protection against the Tribal invaders. In return the people would surrender freedom provisionally and accept the presence of forces on their soil. What people now rebel against is that the Maharaja's accession to India in his position as a fleeing ruler was not sacrosanct and a binding on the people. Mountbatten played a partisan role and did not invoke the article 6 of Amritsar Treaty invalidating the accession.

Kashmir stood out as a beacon of light (Mahatma Gandhi) for peace while the rest of the subcontinent was ravaged in ethnic riots of the partition. India and Pakistan created as two dominions divided their assets and liabilities by consent or force. All the attention now focused on who takes Kashmir? Post colonial governments become replicas of the old imperial order as one ethnic group or other come to dominate the entire region (Katz). Even though anti-imperialist, the nascent democracies sought to uphold the legacy of the empire they inherited. India and Pakistan came out of their colonial shell as juridical sovereign penultimate states. They were not willing to cede territory. Kashmir became a challenge to this legacy. In the meantime people of Kashmir sitting on the fence were deprived of civilian space for democratisation, because ending of the autocratic rule was replaced almost instantly by violence, war, repressive fledgling regimes, anarchy and insurrection. In time the character of the conflict changed, and while the guns were silenced through military impasse and United Nations intervention, a new wave of protest was born. It was now the state against partisans of dissent and an asymmetric conflict was proclaimed as against the war between two nations. The milieu of insurgency sought change in defence of freedom, legitimacy and just order.

British Legacy

There are questions in the minds of people of Kashmir which haunt them. British for all the good they did as their masters, imbedded for over a hundred years in the fabric of their society, nevertheless ought to own up to their part in the culmination of their problems. British cultural singularities were absorbed by the society and a vacuum was felt on their sudden departure. Majority of my own classmates were British children. They all vanished one fine morning in late October 1947, and as I arrived in my school the class was empty. A normative critique of British role in handing over Kashmir to Dogra rule in 1846 and a hundred years later decamping from the colony, leaving behind a conflict, may incriminate them and be asked to redress the losses suffered. Gulab Singh was a cruel warlord who inflicted reprehensible atrocities on people in his totalitarian rule and thereafter by his progeny. Kashmir for a paltry sum was expunged from the polity of Indian dominion.

In retrospect, Kashmir left as a part of British India would have been assigned to its fate in the partition process. Why were the princely states, excluded from the partition? Could these tiny enclaves have survived, left to fend for themselves? In the end of course, they were all swallowed up by force. Close on the heels of partition, the princes were actively exhorted by the

British to assert their independence, construed by cynics as a reward for their collaboration with East India Company in the colonising process. As an end to these means, the princes met their fate and evanesced in disgrace. British rule did not end until June 1948 (Indian Independence Act). Would the British take responsibility for the dispute created during this time? Having left a violent conflict behind, why have the British, as important actors in international politics and head of the Commonwealth nations, not taken an active role in solving the problem since then? Do they disown responsibility altogether, or is it the antics of Machiavellian politics which have failed aspirations of people in Kashmir?

India was a lucrative asset for the Empire. "As long as we rule India we are the greatest power in the world. If we loose it we shall drop straight away to a third-rate power" Lord Curzon, 1901. (Moorhouse) Was there a scorched earth policy at work and Kashmir made the scapegoat, in order to load down their fury ? Great Britain was required to be a party in the accession of Kashmir (Article 6 Amritsar Treaty) and not help in the incursion of armies. Lessons were learnt from this policy replicated in Northern Ireland, Palestine, Fiji, Guyana where non-local army fomented dissent. British by default were responsible for creating the contentious border or Line of Control in Kashmir which kept the conflict going. Stalin adopted a strategy in making arbitrary unaffiliated borders between Armenia and Azers, Uzbecks and Tajiks so that fight ensues and Russia can rule over to keep order (Hobbs). As it happens British made an exit while the conflict was raging. Some exit people of Kashmir say! As laws of international relations become globalised more victims of colonial infraction are coming forward. Ilwa community from Chagos Island, still British, have filed a case against the British for forced migration into Mauritius, where they are suffering. Chagos was used as a nuclear base. Kashmiris may one day piece together enough historical facts to seek justice and atonement. Hopes provide a meaning for existence, it may be their plight and suffering that is recognised by the international community.

The British Government position has always been archetypal of a British diplomacy, a microcosm of their overall political self preservation. One official statement says (Quote 10-11-00) "We are deeply concerned by the continuing conflict in Kashmir and support the search for a just and lasting solution acceptable to the people of Kashmir. We condemn violence and abuse of Human Rights. We continue to urge India and Pakistan to return to bilateral dialogue on Kashmir and the other issues that divide them". What would be the end result of a policy like that ? The Foreign Office never acknowledged their own part in the causes of the conflict or their political obligations to get involved or their active and effective measures they envisage to take in order to make a real impact in a peaceful solution. People of Kashmir are dismayed at their reticent attitude and appalled at their policy of having to toe the line of Americans who have no historical relations with the region or any moral obligations to help.

Part II

Conflict Resolution

 **Introduction:**

The antagonism which underpins the war for control of Kashmir and efforts to manage the conflict takes myriad forms. Learning from despotism of ideas which crystallise opinion, hostility will perpetuate and dominate the positions held by protagonists. It is an established fact that Kashmir dispute has three intrinsic parties involved. It follows therefore that no unilateral or even bilateral solution will hold ground. India has committed a large proportion of its army backed by large amounts of liquid assets to hold on to its positions in Kashmir. Pakistan has over the last half a century disfigured its development programs and lost opportunities to give its people the benefits of a free economy for the sake of its crusades and active military engagement against India over Kashmir. Kashmir and its people have been frozen in space and time with no enhancement in their living standards, now reduced to mere survival levels. All three parties have lost many thousands of precious lives and suffered human rights abuses mankind has ever known. It is therefore a fallacy and a political blunder to exclude anyone of the three protagonists in any facet of peace process or conflict resolution. The autonomy deal passed by Kashmir Assembly for example was rejected by

Indian government but even if it was approved, it would have been a futile exercise because it was completely unilateral and as it happened rejected outright by all three parties. Does it look like a military move using a political tank only serving the purpose of increasing the level of frustration and violence? May be it serves to teach us a lesson, and not to exclude any of the three parties in any proposed attempts at peace making.

As we make progress in our inquiry of a resolution of this ominous conflict , we will examine the factors favourable to this process. We will have reliance on the wisdom of some traditions set out by great philosophers of recent past. The Swiss psychologist Carl Jung wrote, analysing reasons why past events influence behaviour (Modern Man in Search of a Soul 1933), guiding us to think why in the wilderness of violence and strife, many attempts were made to seek peace by the actors in dispute failed. Kashmir itself or its people did not get a credible place in any peace process, the premise being that the dispute is about territory and its affiliation to India or Pakistan, and not between its people and either party. People cry out ! "Why are we used as gambits"." Why is everyone out to hurt us ?" In the event young men of Kashmir lost patience and jumped in the arena. The modus operandi depended on passive resistance, human sacrifices, underground militancy, International support and sketchy political activity. In chapter 5 we will reflect on the limitations of these efforts.

Chapter

❮3❯

Correlates of Peace:
Philosophical Inquiry

'If there is righteousness in the heart, there will be beauty in the character,

If there is beauty in the character, there will be harmony in the home,

if there is harmony in the home, there will be order in the Nation,

If there is order in the Nation , there will be peace (Confucius 551-479 BC).

Peace may not be divisible but in conflicts like Kashmir, it can only be achieved in degrees. Basic tenets of peace making like 'stop fighting, and lay down arms' (Pax) or more complete with cultural and structural freedom, can be achieved by offering alternatives, notwithstanding the nuance of the positions taken by the disputants. People will not compromise on their rights, and for an end to 'Happy Slave', false consciousness (Karl Marx 1818-1883) models of governance. All parties in the dispute are bound to loose something and will feel injustice has been done to them. Negotiations aimed at real peace will assume collaborative (integrative) or win-win situation for all sides. Peace making is one of the noblest of all virtues from Humanism, altruism and religious ethical norms. Shalom is a simple greeting expression in Hebrew and it means peace beyond strife and denotes a destination of complete peace. In the same way Om Shanti signifies peace, peace and peace (Upanishad 1:3:28) in Hindu scriptures. In Islam, peace making is held in supreme regard. God loves those who are equitable (60:8) and those who act in justice (40:9) Qur'an.

Qur'an also stipulates that in making peace 'co-operate in what is good and pious (5:2). In Christian faith peace which passes all understanding for the human soul is promulgated by St Augustine (5th Century AD) and St Thomas Aquinas as achieving the final Kingdom. Although Jesus Christ rejects passivity and acquiescence in dealing with wrong doing, he nevertheless teaches that evil can be opposed without being mirrored. Peace is axiomatic to prosperity and 'progress flows from peace' so sayeth the gospel. Mahayana Buddhism defends reality through direct experiences therefore transcending conceptualisation. We may be mistaking the finger pointing at the moon for the moon itself (Zen). The remarkable discovery of identical 'Y' chromosomes in Jewish and Arab Diaspora posits a thesis that both are children of Abraham and would children of India and Pakistan be so dissimilar that posterity of common heritage become enemies forever. Pyramidal justice bringing rules and norms upon people would apply equally for all.

In our philosophical analysis of the present dissent in Kashmir we have reliance on the ideas of sedition debated by Socrates (469-399 BC). Socrates believed that it is a serious indictment to tell people what kind of a government they should have and give them limited access to plausible alternatives to the way they live. On this moral question he became an apologist for rebellions in the world. He states that the " Unexamined life for a man is not worth living. Politicians who cannot see good from evil, justice from injustice are trivial (Plato).

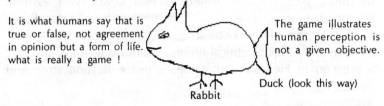

It is what humans say that is true or false, not agreement in opinion but a form of life. what is really a game !

The game illustrates human perception is not a given objective.

Duck (look this way)

Rabbit

The world will associate Kashmir with mountains and lakes which are the centre region of dispute between India and Pakistan. What about looking at Kashmir as an aggregate of individual families? We can see how human perception can be affected by internal picture we create rather than that created by the object. Is that pushing thought beyond limits in order to understand the limits of factual discourse. (Ludwig Wittgenstein 1889-1951)?

Gandhian Perspective compared to Rousseau's Approach

Rousseau (Jean Jacques 1712-78) insisted that in a social contract drawn up, the people were sovereign. Man is born free, but he is in chains everywhere. This thesis formed the basis of the French revolution. Freedom for Rousseau could only be achieved through enforcement of the General Will, to adopt social contract and enforce it. In Kashmir people have now become hardened to believe that their future society must ensure maximum liberty for all in a free and fair democracy. They want an end to authoritarian regimes and parochial attitudes in politics. In their quest for freedom they want to bring in complex political emergency (CPE) to adopt universalism and evolve a consensus as a nation and live in harmony with people of the subcontinent.

Mahatma M K Gandhi (1869-1948) was assassinated by a Hindu extremist, but his spirit lives on across the whole spectrum of Indian society. The world celebrates his teachings on the force of passive resistance and pacifism. A study of Gandhian philosophy is unique in its dispensation of principles which can be adopted to solve Kashmir crisis. I will elaborate on the well known answers given, relevant to our questions in this inquiry.

1.   Mahatma Ghandi believed that 'means are ends in creation'. Application of force on Kashmiris will by implication end in violence and not the peace we are aiming to achieve. Given that the end sought is a social order based on non-

violence and truth, then the means must be characterised by commitment to non-violence and truth. In other words talk to people wilfully as a part of your family.

2.   Satyagraha teaches a firm hold on truth. Should there be an investigation on the claims made by all political groups of Kashmir ?. While as 'Sat' seeks both absolute and relative truth, an inquiry may be in order, to find the rights of the organic civilisation in Kashmir.

3.   Ahimsa was a doctrine Gandhi cherished. It advocated non-violence, minimal harm to others but also non-injury and agape. The question arises: In Kashmir inquiry is any party prepared to suffer in the name of peace and reconciliation and accept compromises and alternate solutions ?

4.   Tapasya: Is anyone prepared to suffer ? Can we make a comparison between the suffering of masses and those who make policies and give orders ?

5.   Objectives of Satyagraha: The clear aim has to be victory over the conflict rather than the opponent, in order to liberate from evil (conflictual forces) and to achieve constructive change of relationships. Translate the belief into practice, the emphasis would rest on negotiations for peace and not on a zero sum contest over military gains between India and Pakistan or militants and security forces.

6.   Stages of Satyagraha: The first step attempts to focus on specific issues responsible for injustices. Having identified the interest, it shares the information with opponent. It is the third stage which also forms the basis of this work where ' Formation of limited goals ' is conceptualised. In other words one has to accept limitations in making targets or finishing lines. The fourth stage is to establish personal contact, and finally only engage in civil disobedience having exhausted all other means. Satyagraha is applicable to states and people alike. In other words military may not go on passive resistance option, they will still restrain themselves from using gratuitous force for the purpose of intimidation and terror.

" Truth resides in every human heart and one has to search for it there and be guided by truth as one sees it. But no one has a right to coerce others to act according to his own view of truth. " " For a non-violent person, the whole world is one

	Durugraha (Power-Orientated)	Satyagraha (Truth-Orientated)
Origin	Unjust situation	Unjust situation
Objective	Overcome opponent: Imposition of correct solution	Convert oppent: End Flexible
Means	Pressure, distruct of opponent coercive non-violence	Help opponent modify position. Faith in integrity of oppenent

family" (Gandhi). There are important clues for resolution of conflict in Kashmir in this passage. Let every party in the dispute be guided by truth. Let us not impose truth on the people of Kashmir, instead enlighten them about events as they unfold in their veracious form. Once violence stops, it obviates the need to erect trenches to protect from each other. We can learn to sum up the courage to love people even though they are imbued in a revolution. When it appeared to him that Indian Government could renege on its promise to transfer assets to Pakistan, Gandhi fasted in order to force India to honour its pledges (Raghavan) Not so for Kashmir in the event of his premature departure, yet one more setback for the ill fated region.

Chapter

◀4▶

Domestic Front

War Without Winners

India and Pakistan are at war for more than half a century now, feuding over who controls Kashmir ? Ever since French revolution, in conflicts like Kashmir, soldiers and non-soldiers all get involved in the war. Territory is controlled by sowing fear and attrition. Everyday people are killed. In ideological terms people of Kashmir have lost faith in any political system offered to them. The complexity of the conflict may be explained by what I term as the myth of half-truths which each protagonist uphold as their declared policy on Kashmir. Pakistan maintains silence on its policy of irredentism and make a case for humanitarian empathy, supporting liberation struggle and self determination for people of Kashmir. India on the other hand remains muted on guarding their tenuous hold over sovereignty by peremptory control over a rebellious insurrection and instead claims to be fighting Pakistani militants for the benefit of the people of Kashmir. These half truths presides over the asymmetric conflict between the state and people who are seen to be defending their corner for legitimacy and order.

The Third party in the conflict are indigenous population who are held in false consciousness in the belief that both rivals are their benefactors. On a political level they are torn between freedom and survival. They have ambivalent loyalties to realist nationalism and liberalism. The political ambience remains deluged with half truths replicating theories of international politics. People, with latent propensity for peace, experience fear of reprisals and uncertain political future. China, one more party in the fray, claims half truth about historical rights over Twang Tract in Tibet and to redraw MacMohan Line over Tibetan border and Silk Road through Aksai Chin. In the meantime they have occupied Aksai Chin, a part of Kashmir, and established at their cost, the legacy of an engineering wonder, the silk road linking Tibet and China. Incidentally, China have announced to build a railway into Tibet meandering through the most challenging terrain in the world.

Fukuyama's panacea of liberalist doctrine would offer people a democratic right to determine their fate. A plebiscite in Kashmir could only be valid if held under supervision of an international monitoring authority. Notwithstanding the fact that this democratic instrument used in similar situations like East Timor and Namibia would find putative defenders, however, it is well known that India stands firmly against involvement of any external actors in the resolution of the conflict. Elections have been held in Kashmir numerous times over the years, giving credence to Kashmir constituent Assembly and marionette regimes, with strings tethered to the New Delhi South Block hierarchy. The conduct of executing such democratic procedures with ballot fixing and intimidation did not alleviate political tensions. There were allegations about the conduct of these elections being rigged and manifestly spurious (Schofield). The resolution passed by this Assembly on 23rd June, 2000, asking for autonomy was rejected outright by India, Pakistan and the local political parties. Indian leaders spurned it because although perpetuity of sovereignty within Indian constitution would remain, the resolution did ask for 1953 position restored wherein Kashmir was a devolved state with only the defence, communication and foreign affairs tied in with India. There is nothing in the core of this resolution for Pakistan or Kashmir's dissident parties and they have dismissed it outright. The only nod of sceptic approval came from JKLF leaders who seek complete independence for unified Kashmir from India and Pakistan, as a step in the right direction.

The primacy of the will of the people is rooted in UDHR Article 21 in which will of the people is the only basis for authority. It may be possible to evolve an egalitarian society based on democratic norms of freedom with their own representative parliamentary government, taken for granted by most other communities of the world. India and Pakistan realised the advantages of mutual amicable relationship and tried to use their finesse of statecraft to resolve the conflict. In the end reliance was placed on force, propaganda, economic hegemony and defining zero sum power struggle to support their respective policies on Kashmir. Two major wars fought were indecisive between the two and ended in a stalemate. Both sides only counted casualties and nothing to show for it.

Notwithstanding the extreme form of suffering, people in Kashmir have proselytised with experience in hard core politics and will accept forward looking liberalist policies. The militants of Kashmir like SWAPO in Namibia fight from the bushes as partisan actors in the dispute. Their frequent encounters with military creates violence and result in the killing fields of Kashmir on a regular basis. Attempts by Indian politicians to seek peace with militants failed. A top Indian politician Mr Jayaprakash Narayan who led an armed revolt against the British occupation of India was disillusioned with the Government for distancing from grassroots (Narayan). There was a ray of hope when Hizbul Mujahidin, the dominating militant group, started peace talks with India. The talks ended with a fractious deadlock over modalities and acceptance of Indian constitution as a prerequisite. In China hard line leaders like Mao Tse-Tung thought about armed resistance as a force to learn lessons from; "Bad things can be turned into good things if an attempt is made, when dealing with militants", he said.

True Cost of Conflict

Cost of the dispute in Kashmir, its perpetuity and violence it breeds can be difficult to assess. It has to be measured not only in terms of the economic development of the region, but also in human terms for its devastating causal effects on life, survival, mental and physical consequences on the population and the social deprivation. If India and Pakistan realise how costly low intensity perpetual war (LIPEW) has been for them over the years, they may be aware of the enormity of depredation of their assets, and perhaps collaborate in peace. Arms purchased in 1992 went up to $12.236 billion. The USA cancelled aid worth $24 million for reported Human Rights abuses.

Russia supplied the bulk of arms worth $ 9364mn and the UK was next on list with arms supply worth $ 1047mn. France, Germany and the USA supplied the rest. The spending on keeping security forces in Kashmir during 1998 to 1999 alone was Rs 60 billion ($ 1.3 bn). Published figure for 2002 is Rs. 50 m an hour. The defence budget of Pakistan during 1992-1993 has been $ 3 billion, a staggering 40 percent of government spending. The Indian Finance Minister made a confession that the defence spending is at 10% of GDP (Zee TV 3rd July, 2000) A credible defence he said is essential for peace in the region. India and Pakistan have locked horns in balance of power politics and this process is self-perpetuating. The amounts expended in imports of major conventional weapons are very excessive and in normal checks and balances of a developing country, the figures would be termed prohibitive both for India and Pakistan. If the two poverty stricken neighbours use the metaphor of the shadow of the future in prisoners dilemma game , they will soon realise zero sum contest means mutual destruction. In order to make an assessment of the cost in terms of purchases of arms the following figures make the point. The conflict has disabled the potential of protecting human needs like personal security, social welfare, basic identity and psychological health. Colossal tangible and intangible assets have been lost to fighting wars and threats of more to come.

1994-98		1993-97	1994	1995	1996	1997	1998	1994/98
Rank-1	Taiwan	Rank-2	731	1162	1451	5311	4756	13311
Rank-2	Saudi Arbia	Rank-1	1298	1249	1961	3292	1948	9748
Rank-7	India	Rank-8	497	932	988	1266	466	4149
Rank-13	Pakistan	Rank-14	683	242	552	614	525	2616
Rank-54	Sri Lanka	Rank-50	56	60	158	42	40	356
Rank-58	Bangladesh	Rank-57	89	126	4	24		243

Recipients of major conventional weapons in South Asia. (Saudi Arabia and Taiwan for comparison). Figures expressed in US $mn at constant (1990) prices.

Can we defend the insensibility we as humans have shown to destruction of our own species ! How can we reconcile to 21 million of us killed in wars since 1945 ? The gruesome figures bring closer to home 15mn in East Asia and 2mn in India, including the 80,000 in Kashmir. It is no surprise that 12 wars were fought on a typical day. There was not a single virtuous day since September 1945 when the world did not have a war on (Burrows).

Kashmir has been classified as a 'violent conflict' region because the number of deaths exceeds 1000. Losses in terms of human lives are estimated at over 65,000 and human development index (HDI) can only be surmised because the most important indicant in a figure would be average life expectancy, apart from literacy and GDP. In Kashmir life expectancy can be very low. An area of 219 sq. km and population of 12 million the population density has been estimated at 50 per sq. km. People treated in hospitals with violence related injuries have been 25,000. Schools burnt during 1992 are 200, shops burnt 3000. Detainees in Indian prisons are estimated at 20,000. (A I).

As if to emulate the big boys, while the US Missile Defence System is taking shape with the new Bush administration and the rest of the world is trying to match up to the challenge, India and Pakistan also overawe each other with their new missiles, capable of longer range and more destructive power. The USA has means and can afford the security pranks, Asians are beavering into the branches, they are perche on.

An unmatched political artefact, a thunderbolt if you like ! Hindus of Kashmir migrated almost as a clean sweep and all 150,000 became refugees overnight. They are housed in camps and living in exile since 1989. Muslims were also forced out of their homes and 10,000 are living in camps in Azad Kashmir. (Cranna 1994). Forced migration is an ongoing process and today as I write 300 villagers including small children walked across the border to Pakistan side of Kashmir, in full view of the army pickets. The migrants complained of intimidation from the border security forces. Was this ethnic cleansing or sanitising a border village ? Repeated and callous pogroms of Sikhs, a relatively safe community, are now being driven out from their homes into exile. Sikhs have played a moderating role and never broken faith with their compatriots. Why then have they been made targets? These are some of the pressing questions, no one has any answers for? Each side has denied responsibility for their cold blooded murders, a position which makes their fate even more uncertain. (ASA 20/24/00 India: A trail of unlawful killings in Jammu & Kashmir: Chitisinghpora and its aftermath). A daunting prospect is rampant use of war tactics in basically a civil conflict. Homes are gutted down repeatedly. " War is Hell " was the doctrine put forth by General Sharman invading Georgia. "Burn everything in sight", he ordered.

Violence in Kashmir is ubiquitous. It has even made inroads into the domestic scene. Violence due to heightened anxiety in political ambience made hard cynics. Kashmiris have become a pariah community. If they travel outside Kashmir, their presence is notified to local police for constant surveillance. They are treated as suspected trouble makers and picked up any time a mishap is reported. Violence has a ripple effect and spreads like wild fire.

Chapter

❮5❯

International Community
and Kashmir

'I believe that the true means of understanding the road to Paradise, is to know that of Hell' (Machiavelli)

In our inquiry of the known factors, we will briefly evaluate the role International community played in the failed attempts at the resolution of the conflict in Kashmir.

United Nations: Each time the United Nations was approached, a negative peace ensued and guns were silenced. Internecine wars were still ravaging the foothills and cities of Kashmir through the fall of 1947 when India approached the United Nations using article 35 of the charter, complaining against Pakistan's aggression in Kashmir. Pakistan made counter charges against India of illegal occupation of parts of Kashmir and unleashing its forces on the indigenous population. The UN intervention included passing resolutions and sending United Nations Commission for India and Pakistan (UNCIP) delegations to the region. All attempts to bring about a plebiscite failed. The UN was used by parties to stop the wars, only to gain time to regroup and fight again.

The United Nations has been criticised for its actions and characterised with a symbolic six and half organisation. Article six giving it the mandate to undertake consensual mediation and stop fighting but stops short half way of article seven if active intervention was required faced with threat to regional peace and security. Article 7 could only be used if supported by a resolution of the Security Council. The remit to act would assume consent by parties in dispute. The UN mediated resolutions came and went with no imprint on the peace process The UNCIP delegations comprised capable mediators like Field Admiral Chester W Nimitz in March 1949 to appointment of A G L McNaughton and then Sir Owen Dixon in September 1950. They all had the mandate to try demilitarise Kashmir and offer options for peace. Each time a deal was agreed, it was thwarted because military withdrawal became the sticking point. The UNCIP teams left the region flustered at the egoistic swagger in all ranks. Kashmir is caught up in a vicarious turmoil in the interface between it and international politics. It is a small nation out in the cold and callous world, while the mores of global society are involved in post cold-war political dynamics and pre-occupations. The UN Motto First 'do no harm' is deceptive.

The UNCIP interventions in Kashmir in a way helped slow motion savagery, because the warring parties were allowed time to regroup, conjure up a new set of military stratagems in the hope the adversary will crack (Hampson). Indo-Pakistani wars blitzed the subcontinent into flames. The UN did not use Article 43 of its charter authorising a standing force to a military response and abate the crisis, nor did the two disputants seek a remedy under article 96 of the charter which would enable the UN to seek opinion of the International Court of Justice. The court would determine if the accession of Kashmir to India by the Maharaja was legal. If the answer was yes, then it would be right for India to accuse Pakistan of being an aggressor. If the verdict was negative, then both countries were guilty of illegal occupation. This route was not adopted by either country for its uncertain consequences.

The UN resolution 98 of 1952 permitted India and Pakistan to maintain a limited force in their respective territories which resulted in agreement by Pakistan keeping 3-6000 troops and India 12-18000 prior to a plebiscite. As will be made known

RESOLUTION	TEXT & ACTION TAKEN	OUTCOME
No 38: (1948): 229th meeting: 17th Jan 1948. Doc. No. S-651	Calls upon India and Pakistan to stop aggravating the conflict.	Full compliance
No.39 (29th. Jan. 1948) 230th session Doc. S-654. By UN Rep. of Belgium	3-member UNCIP selected to investigate facts under article 34 and mediate.	UNCIP try to prepare for plebiscite in both parts of Kashmir. Military observers deployed along borders.
No. 47: (21st April 1948) 286th session Doc. S-726 By Belgium, Canada, China Columbia, USA and UK jointly.	Satisfaction: Both India and Pakistan desire an impartial plebiscite. UNCIP increased to five members.	Conditions that India will keep some army during plebiscite and pro-Indian local government would stay, was rejected by Pakistan. India agreed to the proposal.
No. 51: (3rd June 1948): 312 Session Doc. S-819. Submitted by Syria.	Reaffirms resolutions No's 38 and 47. Instructs UNCIP to continue the task.	India refused the appointment of a plebiscite administrator.
UNCIP resolution (5th Jan. 1949) Doc. S-1196.	Chester W Nimitz appointed as the plebiscite administrator. Proposed: USA	India refused and pleaded that Pakistan must be treated as an invader, not at Par.
President AGL, McNaughton: 457th meeting of Security Council. 22nd Dec 1949	Preserve agreements, demilitarise and conduct plebiscite.	Proposal refused by India.
No, 80 (14th March 1950) proposed by Cuba, Norway, UK, USA. Doc.S-1469	Calls upon India and Pakistan to execute demilitarisation within five months in accordance with McNaughton proposal.	Karachi agreement (27th July 1949). War stopped after one year negotiations. No agreements reached on demilitarisation.
No 91: 30th March 1951. submitted by UK and USA. Doc. No S-2017-Rev.	Decides to appoint success or to sir Owen Dixon. Calls for arbitration.	India refuses a mediator's role in the dispute.

No. 96 (10th Nov.1951) Doc.S-2392.	Dr Frank Graham's report. Proposals for demilitarisation and plebiscite.	Stalemate
No. 98: (23rd Dec. 1952) adopted in the 611th meeting. Doc. S-2883	Recalling Resolution 91 and UNCIP Res. of 5th Jan 1949 which was accepted by both India and Pakistan	Pakistan did not participate in the voting stalemate continues.
No.122 (24th Jan. 1957, adopted at the 765 the meeting.	Reaffirms any action taken by Kashmir Assembly to align with India would not constitute a disposition of the state.	USSR abstains. UN decides to continue its deliberations of the dispute.
No. 123: 21st Feb. 1957) adopted at the 774th session.	Requests the president from Sweden to visit the subcontinent and examine reality.	Resolution passed. USSR abstaining.
No. 126 (Dec. 1957) 808th meeting.	Mr. Gunner Jarring reports on his return from India and Pakistan that both recognise and accept resolution 38 for a plebiscite.	No further action taken. Stalemate.
18th May 1964 (1117th meeting, the president (French) concludes.	Debated juridical status of Kashmir and principles of charter applicable.	Kashmir question remains on the agenda
No.1172 (6th June 1998) adopted at the 3890 meeting.	Reaffirming statement of its president of 14th May 1998 S-PRST-98-12 and of 29th May S-PRST-17 after the Nuclear tests by both India and Pakistan. Article 4 urges the parties to show restraint. UN recognised that the core of the conflict was the undecided Kashmir dispute. (A-5)	Urges dialogue between the two. The article 6 welcomes efforts of Secretary General and 15 requests him to report steps taken by India and Pakistan to implement the present resolution.

later, the reduction in forces was a ploy used to derail the peace process. In my sketches for a solution I have assumed that a small presence of forces from both countries would have to be received with finesse.

Summary of United Nations Resolutions passed on Kashmir dispute and their outcome. (See page 45 and 46).

Western Powers: *   The western countries tried to help in solving the blistering conflict and the only tangible way out which seemed politically correct was to suggest a plebiscite under supervision of independent observers.** This blueprint has been used in other situations but in Kashmir the sticking point in demilitarisation by India and Pakistan was especially about who withdraws first ? The last ten years' violence and an anarchical system made a plebiscite even more difficult to achieve. On a legal take, one would be faced with the Indian constitution, article 1 of which states that Kashmir is an integral part of India and elections were held under the umbrella of this act. The move was received by the international community with cautious optimism. "We (U.S. authorities) have a policy which is continuing and has not changed on the Kashmir question. While Washington's call for bilateral talks can perhaps be taken as a renewed recognition of the efficacy of the Simla Accord, it will be rash to see these views, attributed to a U.S. official, as an American endorsement of the Indian position that the ensuing elections would stabilise the situation in Jammu and Kashmir". HINDU: 21st August, 1996.

---

*   United Nations Resolution 1264 authorising multinational forces to stop fighting in Dilli, East Timor, was a success story as described by Richard Hallbrook, the United States envoy. " This is how UN is supposed to work, as envisaged by Churchill and Roosevelt". In September, 1999 Kofi Annan, Secretary General, said " It is difficult to find money for medicines, but easy to find for coffin. We know what needs to be done. What is now needed is the foresight and political will to do it".

**   The point is that the United States and the Soviet Union had more than one narrow escape. India and Pakistan have even less margin for error than the U.S. and USSR did over Cuba and Berlin -- if only for geographical reasons, since no ocean separates India and Pakistan. Moreover, during the half century of the cold war we and the Soviets never shed a drop of each other's blood on the battlefield, at least not in direct combat. India and Pakistan, by what I think is a very germane contrast, have over approximately the same span of time fought three wars, and there continue to be frequent and sometimes fatal exchanges of artillery fire across the line of control in the disputed territory of Kashmir. And then there's the economic dimension of security. Before India and Pakistan decide to replicate the U.S. and Soviet nuclear competition, they should look very hard at the price-tag. A recent Brookings study estimated that maintaining the nuclear capability of the United States costs this country just under five and a half trillion dollars. (Brookings: Talbot 1998 Nov.12).

A moiety of the United States policy over Kashmir has been diplomacy. Mr Clinton had the Kargil war ended, so Indo-Pakistan dialogue can resume. The USA maintains that Kashmir is a contentious issue (Raphael) and needs urgent resolution. (Brookings). Visiting India in March 2000, Mr Clinton offered mediation to resolve the conflict if asked, a gesture construed as a politically correct response which is replicated by other western leaders. Mediation, it may be argued, is a help towards bringing to surface a consensus between disputants. In reliance on that premise it is no use repeating this remedy when consensus is what is wanting between the parties. We have to set this bias against what transpires behind close doors. What matters in the end is the agenda on Kashmir in foreign policy offices round the western world. It is worth observing that the apologist for the state administering control over an insurrection, the terrifying assumptions made are that state control of a revolt against sovereign authority, humanity is a mere tool to bend subjects to compliance. China as an example has Tiananmin Square thrown at its face, every time political leverage is sought. When the right time came, China agreed to bend because WTO membership and Preferred Nation Status was on offer. Human Rights took a back seat. Greedy sectors of the West claim to abhor violence at the same time as selling arms to feuding parties, which protracts conflict and violence.

Commonwealth has been in conformity with the United States policy on Kashmir. They have offered their good offices to help with a dialogue should both parties agree. It may not come as a surprise that this rhetoric takes you on a tour of de-ju-vo and discovery of covert salience from Western hierarchy. It may be argued that Commonwealth organisation with its organic roots in colonialism, still has strands of the imperium dominating its agenda setting and politics. Taking lead from current events, it is worth observing the attitude of Mr Don McKenan, the new secretary general, towards military regime in Pakistan. Not one word about Kargil episode, the underlying cause for military taking over power, but there was recrimination and repeated glee portrayed by McKenan on Pakistan's suspension from the Commonwealth. He was happy for issues from Zimbabwe and Fiji Island to fester with inactivity.

This obsession with democracy whichever form it takes, whether or not it is radical, guided, liberal or consociational, dominates the politics of Commonwealth. What we witness here is prophesied triumphalism of democracy as a panacea for all ills. Democracy is accepted even if it becomes a vehicle for temporising with the murder of white farmers by war veterans of Zimbabwe or diluted forms of state terrorism paraded. In the world of realism there would be little room for Commonwealth especially in preference to a strong regional organisation who will stand up to the challenges of global anarchy.

USSR: After the end of 1965 India-Pakistan war, the Soviet Union, having realised its hegemonic position was getting undermined in the region, felt it should play a role in reconciliation. Prime Minister Alexia Kosygin offered mediation which was rejected by both India and Pakistan, nevertheless arranged for the two countries to stop the war and meet in the Russian city of Tashkent. On 3rd January, 1966, Indian Prime Minister Mr Shastri and President Ayub of Pakistan met and agreed to resolve the Kashmir dispute and withdraw forces to their positions before the war. Mr Shastri died next day of a heart attack, and the peace process with him. Indira Gandhi took over as PM and the treaty was stalled.

Non-governmental Organisations

Organisation of Islamic Countries (OIC 97) has made pleas for peace and resolution of Kashmir dispute in accordance with the wishes of the people, and offered help. The 50-member organisation promote Islamic solidarity and help with social, economical and political matters. They have come out against terrorism and fundamentalism. OIC played a decisive role in promoting negotiations which ended hostilities in conflicts like the one between Moro Nationalists and Philippines government. The organisation is making concerted efforts at resolution of conflict in Afghanistan and Central Asian countries. They invited Kashmiri leaders to participate in discussions over Kashmir dispute which is a standing issue on their agenda in all their meetings. In the end the Kashmiri leaders were prevented from attending. The organisation has adroit politicians in its executive and would be suitable intermediaries in the event of being accepted by their mutual friends, India and Pakistan.

Soros Foundation and Freedom House have come strong in defence of the rights of vulnerable people like those in Kashmir. The new Association of Asian Parliaments for Peace (AAPP) created by parliamentarians of 31 countries at a meeting in Bangladesh in September, 1999 may have a remit to influence the peace process in Kashmir. International Human Rights organisations like Amnesty International, Asia Watch, Physicians for Human Rights and United Nations Human Rights Commission have publicised violation of Human Rights and gratuitous violence on civilians and on that basis campaigned for political reconciliation and peace. NGOs focussed on Kashmir are spread all over the world. They play a vital role in disseminating information on a daily basis, circulation of literature round the political world. Organisation for South Asian Peace **(OSAP)** helping with this publication is based in the UK and has the support of moderate peace campaigners from the subcontinent. OSAP has espoused a radical approach in resolution of the difficult conflict in Kashmir by offering a pragmatic inventory of options available to India, Pakistan and people of Kashmir. Nearly 500 delegates from India and Pakistan defied the pressures by their governments including ultra nationalist forces and participated in the Fifth Joint Convention of Pakistan-India Peoples' Forum for Peace and Democracy held on April 6-8, 2000, in Bangalore. This would be seen as the foundational concrete to build on the process of peace. The participants renewed their pledge to work for peace and adopted the Bangalore Declaration and a Resolution on Kashmir calls upon Governments of India and Pakistan to order cessation of all hostilities directly and indirectly, the various militant organisations of Jammu and Kashmir to eschew violence, the Government of India to release all political detainees, so that the peoples of all sections of Jammu and Kashmir can decide their future in a democratic manner. It espouses to achieve reconciliation, and exhorts India, Pakistan and of the peoples of Kashmir to strive together to find a solution acceptable to the peoples of Jammu and Kashmir and the sub-continent (HTML Document Encodingutf-8). Womens' Peace Initiative in South Asia (India) have established two centres for widows in Jammu and Anantnag in Kashmir and have come out openly for a dialogue between India, Pakistan and Kashmir to resolve the dispute in Kashmir which has given birth to a nation of political widows on a very large scale.

Chapter

<6>

Limitations

Conceptual analysis of the contemporaneous COOL behaviour from the West towards resolution of the conflict in Kashmir and the end of cold war.

1989 celebrated truimphalism over collapse of communism epitomised in Fukuyama's 'End of History' doctrine As if by design, about the same time violence spread in the streets of Kashmir like wild fire. Jammu Kashmir Liberation Front (JKLF), a local insurgent group declared open war against the Indian armed forces stationed in Kashmir. This was happening while Francis Fukuyama was writing his treatise about western liberal democracy winning over all other ideologies of the world including Communism, Fascism and Islamic rule. In his futuristic dream he overlooked some of the intensely visceral conflicts still heaving in Kosovo, Palestine, Kashmir, Rwanda, and Sri Lanka disfiguring the map of the world politics. Having expressed his vision he stated that " We are not condemned to live forever in the Realist world of inevitable conflict ". Fukuyama argued that at the level of Political ideas as against economy, individuals' struggle to be recognised by others has come to an end with triumph of liberalism. Having reliance on this premise from standpoint of South Asian politics, the question arises, whether any liberal democratic regime in the region exists actually.

A commonly held perception in political circles is that if sufficient reason compelled the West to act, a way would be found to resolve the Kashmir conflict. Answers to these questions are disturbing and worth deliberating on in some detail. In the New World Order America has no need to establish allies or foreign bases. There would be no reason to have an air base in Pakistan aimed against Russia or China. The USA is the sole super-power and wants other countries of the world to assume their own security capability so that the USA will relax their universal hegemonic grip. (Kissenger). The policy towards small conflicts like Kashmir is to keep a distance and make use of the Peace Agencies. It would be ingenuous to expect the USA to step in and make a plausible impact on the Peace Process without using its power to influence outcome. That would be far fetched in view of the two declared NATO doctrines, and post September II world politics.

1.   The first policy is to contain Islamic Green Menace now that the soviet empire has been vanquished. Unfortunately for no fault of the local secular population, Kashmir has been included in the Islamic extremist belt by far right politicians which extends in their view from Hisbolah in Lebanon to Iran, across Central Asia, Xingiang and Afghanistan to militant groups fighting Indian security forces in Kashmir. The reality would be far removed with an appraisal of casualties in Kashmir over the decades of conflict. It is by accounts of statistics produced by Indian agencies that the bulk of militants killed or held in prisons are the local youth not seen as fundamentalist elements in the society.

2.   The second policy is to discourage self-determination and creation of new states. The idea was first conceived by Douglas Hird Ex-British Foreign Secretary when dealing with Eastern Europe. This policy has now been adopted by NATO across the board and has an impact on Kashmir. The idea stems from security concerns for NATO from emergence of new countries. The new states may need to be kept contained, with increased commitment to cost.

There is a ground breaking inquiry into how misperceptions about the East were used to develop an ethno-centric rationale in order to justify imperialism, beyond the clichés and stereotypes of terrorism and barbarism (Saiid). In the mistaken application of their own norms, there is a perception in the West that 'democratic Peace Theory ' is a panacea for resolving disputes. This liberalist view is owned by Ex. President of USA, Mr Clinton, in the belief as stated that democracies do not fight wars with each other and in theory each time Pakistan gets a military government, peace efforts by the West are halted. Unfortunately the Kantian ideals are not met with 'democratic peace theory' as applied to Kashmir. Even reinstating a semblance of democracy brings more violence in the streets and visible coercion to either bring people to vote in elections or prevent them from doing so. The presence of standing armies and violence is synominous with fear.

Mr Clinton visiting South Asia in March 2000, was seen to have tamed down his normally liberalist policy on Kashmir. Did he waver on his altruistic agenda because of his short term in office or a risk he may be taking to impede the presidential campaign in support of Al Gore ? A tilt in favour of Pakistan would in real terms and in equal measure be a tilt against India. Equipoise treatment would end in stalemate which in the event caused suffering for people of Kashmir. Strong element of right wing nationalism and pragmatism is deep rooted in American politics and Mr Clinton was too astute a politician to ignore the trends. Utilitarianism to Clinton was like cost and benefit exercise is to an economist. The other constraint for Mr Clinton was the NATO policy of not supporting creation of new states, especially so if they have a dominant Muslim content. Mr Clinton is a genius with innovation. It is possible he carried a few ideas in his pocket for Kashmir ! Did he ever get a chance to pull one out ? For all the sumptuous hospitality he enjoyed, he floundered in the end.

Have America and other western countries got it wrong ? Should they adopt this parochial defensive attitude against supporting self-determination of states where insurrection has cost thousands of lives ? Sceptics will critique this approach and instead call for a better understanding of the real issues of discord involved. The western liberal philosophy is founded on the maxim laid down by president Woodrow Wilson (1856-1924) who upheld the ideal of self-determination. Is there enough ground for a change of that policy ? How realistic is the fear that the Green Arc of Jihad is spreading across, Hisbollah, fighters in Caucasus, Xinjiang or Mujahidin operating across Afghanistan, Pakistan and Kashmir ? It is argued that nature of conflict in each of these regions has indigenous roots and each one has a causal relation to its own political background. The prevailing western fear of Islamic Menace has been challenged by the French academic Jaques Derrida. He expressed concern on West's categorisation of Islamic world. The cultural identity is often expressed as the fanatical characteristics of the Islamic fundamentalism and until the cold war Eastern Europe was regarded with similar distrust. This, Derrida described as 'logo-centricism' of western thought which I believe has implication for Kashmir. It is possible fundamentalism is creeping into Kashmir arguably ascribed to peremptory sentences imposed on people, which in turn, have reached a critical mass. In all these years of rebellion in Kashmir, no one has ever heard a slogan saying "Save Islam " and yet western media always refer to the uprising as Muslims against predominantly Hindu India. It is debated if such inept coverage of the troubles in Kashmir will help in eliminating conflictual situations and attempts at making peace.

We are now in the year 2002 on a watershed of South Asian politics. Americans have stepped in to avert war between India and Pakistan so as not to divert attention from anti-terrorist coalition. India has taken a war posture against Pakistan so that militant activity in Kashmir subsides and the insurrection will die down. Elections to the local assembly would assume a democratic facade and a semblance to normalcy. There are other factors at play. There are billions of dollars worth orders for military hardware pending execution in the UK and USA for both India and Pakistan. If permanent peace prevails, these orders will be redundant causing hardship to work force in defence industries of the donor countries.

Part III

Dialectics of Kashmir Dispute

 Introduction:

It follows from empirical analysis of the impediments to a solution in Kashmir dispute that complexity which surrounds it is worth a scrutiny. If progress has to be made, reliance can be placed on a system of dialectics as devised by German philosopher George Hegel (1770-1831) in which opposing ideas have been synthesised. In Kashmir the starting point or thesis is resolution of the conflict caused by claims and counterclaims and limited understanding of the real issues at stake. Sooner or later the peace process comes to a stop and throws its opposite, the violence. This becomes the antithesis. It is only when superior understanding of the dispute which takes into account the needs for a solution is in place that progress or synthesis can be achieved.

In the ensuing paragraphs a reference has been made to the profound outcome the conflict has on the population of Kashmir and the subcontinent. The aim of the exercise is application of dialectics to analyse the nature of challenges before peace makers. Violence or antithesis, it is argued, not only stalls the progress but also makes peace or synthesis a far cry unless the attempts at conflict resolution put in place are understood and their limitations have been fully realised. One such flaw is the misconception in the West of terrorism and Islamic fundamentalism playing any part in Kashmir. The accusation it will be argued has not been investigated in detail and a deductive logic applied became a convenient instrument of understanding. A public debate or an open media polls if initiated would, it is proposed, have altered the preconceived notions (Mode 1995). We will first reflect on the magnitude of suffering followed by the ominous side effects like nuclear threats and terrorism. A brief dialectical analysis concludes the topic.

Chapter

‹7›

Impact of Conflict on People of Kashmir

Where are we? Where have we come from? Where do we go from here? (Hegel)

How do Kashmiris perceive their present life ? Rooted in the past, striving for the good of posterity in future, they remain anxious, because the society is a partnership between those who are living, those who are dead and those who are to be born.(Edmund Burke 1729-1797). It may be expedient to contextualise the normative feelings people are caught up in and what hopes they cherish for future in view of the egregious rights violations they face. Incidents of humiliation and suffering are reported on a daily basis, epitomising the political landscape. Notwithstanding the hand grenade attacks, sniper killings, surprise military attacks and violence from all sides, people subsist on a tenuous thread of twilight existence in the hope of a better future. The economy of Kashmir is in shambles like a dusty storm. There is political money in circulation from unknown sources. The money dissipates in frantic consumerism and inflation. It is not invested in sustainable development projects. It creates a sensation by its spectacle, increasing deprived social class. There is no inward investment into Kashmir. All the money India allocates, by multinationals just pays wages, if that at times. Economy in real terms has crashed. A new dispensation with structural and social justice tied up to politics, the drudgery of their life is under siege (Newbury).

People ask, "Are these exotic Himalayan mountains created by God, a setting for fighting wars ?" A comprehensive exposition is sought from within the heartland of the society. Where have we gone wrong? Are we the people that did not take the Arc of Noah and are perhaps drowning now? Who are we deluged by political and social incursions? Are we now faced with a future of hyphenated identities? Like Indian-Kashmiri, Pakistani-Kashmiri, Chinese-Kashmiri or may be akin to the lost tribes of Moses with no moorings. Answers elude them. Have these subjects of God's Kingdom got protection under a bill of Rights? Statutory Protection would be guaranteed by legislative laws or entrenched in a written constitution, similar to the ten amendments of the US constitution which they fall back on for civil liberties and freedom.

Having regard to the theory of causal relations, repeated episodic incursions make them wonder if their natural scenic countryside is responsible for all their troubles. People instinctually identify themselves with ambiance of freedom in nature. Nature is free, because you can breathe and roam in the wilderness and be subsumed. Dynamism in life pulsates in society demanding changes in order to establish the thread linking the ephemeral to the eternal. In other words, their own lives depend on how they blend in with the architecture of Supreme order. India and Pakistan will therefore have to submit to the cries of 'Freedom' emerging from the grassroots of these people or make changes in the attitudes governing relationships. Do people consider the state ruling them an actuality of the ethical idea? It has to be assumed from the quantum of sacrifices made by people that the concept of revolution which pervades the society is axiomatic to their survival. Determinism, after all, proposes that all events are the result of previous causes 'The billiard ball view'. It is not religion. What else could it be? Interactive conflict resolution activities matching to the current conditions and recent events in the conflict will clear the air to make progress. Kashmir is Heaven on fire with a disaster looming at every corner for the natives every day of their lives. The local regimes have been accused of corrupt practices and misplaced loyalties. A handful of families have shared power, a system construed as an oligarchic rule with little credibility. Such a state could not be relied upon for the protection of its people's lives and basic civil rights. It follows that in practice the elite in governments over extend their powers for self-preservation and depend upon the endurance of the people they rule to provide the means to that end. In other words if there were no people to keep under control, there would be no loyalties shown by extra display of force. Constituent assembly in Kashmir was believed to be an instrument of guided democracy. Confidence in public participation was a far cry. Indian media reported mixed stories of coercion and cooperation in elections held earlier. In the meantime people believe that their purgatory is destined for them as the side effect of a revolution. Revolution for them is salvage from suffering and a better life for future.

Revolution they say has the right ingredients for them. They take comfort from political movements in history, as described by the Italian optimist Giuseppe Mazzini (1805-1872). This optimism is offset by the present transformation the society is experiencing in sociological terms and physical and mental well being. The suffering is proving too onerous for them*.

People endure the suffering in the hope of better days to come. In the tumultuous history of Kashmir, its natural scenic beauty lured even the covetous occupiers to build in Kashmir in order to heighten its beauty, infrastructure, gardens and other

---

*A   traveller from USA in Kashmir describes his experience. " Outside the town of Pattan (Kashmir) I pass a car that has been stopped at a check point. In front of his whole family, wife, children and his mortified mother, the driver is squatting down and hopping. " **Like a rabbit** ". The police shouts at him " Jump like a rabbit ". I asked the officer, what was going on? " When asked him to pull over for a search. The man didn't comply quick enough" the officer replied. The driver, a well dressed man in a new Maruti Sedan car stares far into the distance, his face a mask of stone. He keeps hopping. The officer has not asked him to stop. {Blank 1999}. After dusk every major road has check posts, intercepting every car and searching anyone venturing out at that time.. This practice is in force for over ten years and makes life very onerous for the civil society.

tourist facilities. The political turbulence it is going through now has not only devastated those assets but also docked all efforts to any further development, in keeping with the rest of the world's tourist resorts.

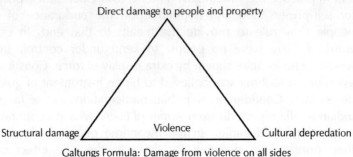

Galtungs Formula: Damage from violence on all sides

The social unrest riding roughshod on their lives caused health problems to such proportions that existing medical facilities cannot cope. One of the singularities of civil war and guns in the streets is driving people indoors. The resources for sustenance cannot cope with increasing population from 4 million in 1947 to an estimated 12 million now residing in this war torn country. It is a social anomaly that people dying fast and constantly under threat of death also seem to procreate generously ! Euphemistically, Call it the 'New York power-cut phenomenon'. Blackouts outside leads to activity indoors. It was rare for a Kashmiri to consider migration as his salvation even if they travelled far afield. Now there are an estimated 2 million people living as diaspora round the world. They all have strong emotional strings tugging at their hearts towards a return home. Nostalgia for them is unbearable. They miss the ambience of tranquillity, the icicles dripping water from roof verges, the fainéant lifestyle with long robes hiding the fire-pot (Kangri). which is their mobile central heating and a hearty sense of humour which dominates social discourse. In the realistic world however while the world has moved on to an era of post-modernism with a cultural and intellectual shift to modern society, Kashmiris are entrenched in seeking identity and a position in the world society.

October 2002 the common man in Jammu and Kashmir was still under a cloud of overbearing rule by the National conference government in which militarism towers above all else in local administration, backed up by atavistic belief in heroism and legitimacy as an instrument of government policy. Higher echelons of power imbue the societies with fear of retribution and misplaced loyalties. It left people alarmed and outraged. It also troubles people to find the concept ingrained in their minds of being a non-entity pariah community. There is evidence that they are indomitably set out to change that image and not to worship nemesis idols but make their rights known. Confronted with the spectacle of carnage, rape, orgies of violence, authorised by civilised echelons of power, people cynically believe that political culture is as close to barbarism as polished iron is to rust (a drop of water being enough to make it appear). It may be appropriate to conclude the topic with a memorable quote from the works of the Irish poet W. B. Yeats (1865-1935):

'Too long a sacrifice, can make a stone of the hearts.'

Chapter

◀8▶

Human Rights Fifty Years On

The World which seems to lie before us like a land of dreams,
So various, so beautiful, so new,
Hath really neither joy, nor love, nor light, No certitude, nor
peace, no help for pain,
And we are here as on a darkling plain,
Swept with confused alarms of struggle and flight, Where
ignorant armies clash by night.
(Mathew Arnold ; Dover Beach)

A glimpse into Human Rights in Kashmir through the eyes of an affected bystander is indicative of the magnitude of human suffering. In my search for guidance from empirical and normative wisdom, I have set out to demonstrate that peace in Kashmir is possible and that the longer we procrastinate the more suffering will be inflicted on the people at large. In the time that the United Nations has been instilling precepts of Rights into the realm of international politics and celebrating the progress made in the fifty years from universal declaration for human rights convention, Kashmir has experienced a consistent erosion of rights, from the autocratic rule to oligarchy and ongoing harsh treatment of innocent citizens. I do not wish to chronicle the abuses of Human Rights, a subject very extensively covered by International organisations and human rights activists from the subcontinent and the world (Siraj). I want to simply dedicate these few pages in making feelings known expressed in each event as a little poem. My own observations tainted with my medical background foresee a gloomy outcome for the future of victims, especially those sexually abused. The little poems have a resonance in their cadence of dehumanising experiences.

"The will of the people shall be the basis of the authority of government." UDHR Article 21 (1&3)

Does Universal Declaration on Human Rights need re-writing? Great Britain may adopt the European Human Rights Law; they have floundered their ethical foreign policy in favour of trading for money soaked in blood. In law and order related to human rights, could intense treatment of citizens be justified ? Apologists for the peremptory rule say force is used to protect the innocent. Is that the factual image ? What laws guide the governing practices in Kashmir ? If we celebrate the postulates of Jeremy Bentham's view that 'Right is the child of law and real laws come from real rights' (Cranston), it is a horrifying thought that in Kashmir the basic right to life is a question mark on every human head alive. There is a clear disjuncture between theory and practice of International law.

For my reckoning these laws may have the elegance of legal jargon and organisational theory, they have little relevance to the events in the streets of Kashmir. Banality of evil as described by Hanna Arendt (1906-75) is sporadic as evidenced by universal impunity in criminal behaviour. It was exemplified by Eichman's deposition in Jerusalem, wherein he claimed to be a dutiful citizen, carrying out orders for genocide of Jews. Rape became a weapon of war. 'Kill these scum babies' was the caption on newspapers 'Hundreds of women were found wandering the hills, drugged, half naked and half crazed'. How many then gave birth is impossible to know (Kosovo rapes- 16-04-2000 Observer). It follows from the analysis of events in Kashmir that the role of interests, power and hegemony takes precedence in governance. Endless hurricane of violence sweeps across all sections of the society especially the innocent.

Gods' egalitarianism :- ' You are no safer travelling first class '

It seems a paradox of normative justice that nowhere else can you find an apparently democratically protected society being subject to the vagaries of rule trusted completely to the sinews of militarism. Unfortunately this brings in a total fear which pervades the lives of all citizens. In Kashmir today, those who choose to be a part of ruling apparatus get killed, those who defy the political order get killed, those who cherish human rights get killed, those who are ingenuous observers also get killed in crossfire if not by design. That of course does not account for the armed combatants from all sides, who die every day in large numbers and get a mention in the media as an item of routine news. Has Kashmir now turned into a human abattoir and a coliseum of human suffering ?

Massacre in cold blood of innocent families who mind their own business in their own time challenges rationality. How do you reconcile with banality of evil as exhibited in pogroms of Chitisingpora and Anantnag or the Hindu pilgrims travelling to Amarnath Cave in Kashmir on a sacred mission. (Attacks and bombings on the civilian population, inflicting incalculable suffering especially on women and children shall be prohibited and such acts shall be condemned. So spells out the General Assembly Resolution 3318 (XXIX)-1 of 14 December, 1974. Women as legal subjects are equal citizens, presumed to have given a notional consent to social contract to be governed, nevertheless find themselves vulnerable to abuse. They get molested, killed, raped, intimidated and left bereaved in destitution. As if designed for target practice, their feet get shot at by their own brothers for not covering their face with Hijab. Women are seen in thousands satting outside police stations enquiring about their disappeared sons or husbands. Estimated 2000 young people are missing (A I) presumed to be either held incommunicado or killed in custody without a name assigned to them. I have made a feeble attempt at translating some of the testimonies from victims of tyranny endemic in all parts of Kashmir. The sad stories unfolding to a predetermined end in the cadence of little poems.

Miriam in prayer

Every morning I woke
through my growing years

I mused, I laughed, I had
no fears

I looked out yonder at
the rising sun

With a burgeon mind for
bliss and fun

A glimpse of light, hopes
and fears

Youth and delight my
body bears

Then one dreadful night

An awesome thunder,
shearing skies

Doors crashed with rav-
ing cries

Soldiers O God! angry
and vile

A pack of wolves, rank
and file

Ripped were clothes by a
thousand hands

Clawing nails, the ani-
mals, the fiends

Snarling mouths and fe-
line teeth

A mountain of bodies, I
lay beneath

My Day of judgement, a
world of bane

Lynched in torment,
soothing in pain

Clubbed and gagged I re-
signed to die

Those beautiful roses,
wilted they lie

(MS)

It was the ominous night of Nov 4/5 1997 when 20 innocent women were gang raped in the Qunel village of Qaziabad Kupwara Kashmir. Power driven men embarked on a premeditated ruse of humiliation. Such atrocities are rooted in history. In the Raj days women were raped in tea plantations, railway carriages and on board steamers. The helpless victims either died or preferring death to dishonour committed suicide. (Winin)

Zooni's testimony

Stormy blast, my ears did hark

Hearing in distance, steps in dark

Big boots approaching rattling windows

Brandishing guns, gruesome shadows

The bestials shouting, bringing doom

smashed their way, into my room

They hit me, shoved me on the ground

Tore my clothes, they tied me down

I lay struggling, my body was bare

stifled and gagged, there was no air

Out of body, I see me dying

Writhing, bleeding, fighting, crying

An abyss it was I plunged so deep

Flames of Hell, storm and sleep

If I live, a corpse will I be,

This incubus will not set me free

(MS)

The suffering of raped victims does not stop with the experience of the atrocity itself. They become a life-long casualty of social and medical problems. They are ostracised socially and live a very lonely life. They carry the stigma of unwanted pregnancies and disease.

Social Widows

Where do I turn? Where do I go?
Never did I folly, No blemish to show

I have cried in agony, I wanted to die
Nights were dreary days went by

Burden of life has crouched my back
Ending my life? The courage I lack

Where do I turn? Where do I go?
Your world of justice, Does anyone know?

(MS)

Husbands shame was mitigated by help from the community and reassuring them. It was the unmarried girl victims who suffered most. Who will marry a girl who lost her virginity and was molested in this way! A lot of women have since left their husbands. Others have been under treatment for physical and mental illnesses. Girls dreaming to acquire the art of living, now learn techniques of existence.

Reminiscing, I thought in my madness
I cherished and loved al my dreams
My world of sighs and hopes, it seems

All those years of tumble and play
The laughs I got, night and day

A restive surge of joy and delight
The dawn was end of a lovely night

Oh! my gorgeous life, where art thou gone!
The cartiffs, wrenched and left me torn

(MS)

Children grow up with vivid, strident echoes of screams from their mothers and sisters being gang-raped. The experience makes deep furrows in their minds reflected in future years as hardened militant behaviour even in their social lives. Rape has been the most pervasive feature of structural and cultural violence in Kashmir with grave knock on effects which will ravage the society for years to come. (In Kashmir a pattern has emerged of harassment of those who are critical of the government ; A I: June 00)

Collateral Damage

Vicarious retribution is common practice in Kashmir. Most of the victims are innocent bystanders and most vulnerable. I will beg indulgence in quoting a tale from the writings of Jalaludin Rumi (Persian philosopher) ' A shopkeeper kept a parrot in his shop. One day a cat overturned a vessel of oil and fled. When the merchant came back he thought the bird had spilt the oil and struck him so hard that all his feathers fell from his head. Some time later, seeing a bald man passing by, the parrot called out " What oil did you spill ? ".

The impressionable youth have been assimilating the ravages of this war and will grow up as partisans in politics, either delinquent as social rebels or outright militants.

Young Witness (Age 7)

Mom Mom, please don't cry!
Just beckon me so, for you I die

I see your eyes through your tangled hair
They are red and drenched, I cannot bear

You know I love you as never before
My body shakes, my heart is sore

So kind, so gentle, why was it you
My beautiful angel what can do?

Are you in agony? It hurts me too
Should I be running, or die with you

I will fight to my end to ease your pain
Restore your honour, your selfhood again

I will give my life to vanquish my goal
I will destroy the evil, to ease your soul

Mom Mom have faith in your child
Blood will flow, to avenge our pride

(MS)

Nuclear Arms/Terrorism & Kashmir

Let us be aware of the facts that the spectre of nuclear war haunts these poorest nations of the world, not so as to denounce the trigger happy nature of the two arch rivals but because the phantom of galloping demography and ensuing hunger threatens the subcontinent, and one more unjust war is ominously round the corner. While defence minister of India talks in terms of 'flexible response (NATO doc. MC14/3) with option of 1st nuclear strike to halt aggression and force withdrawal of advancing Pakistani army. Did he ever consult experts to find out the magnitude of disaster from fallout of radiation even with an air-burst explosion?

Examination of the world wired up to the web of nuclear arms, is expected to make a connection of the anarchic race of these lethal weapons and an impasse over Kashmir dispute. It is argued that India and Pakistan have hardened their attitude towards reconciliation since both made a show of their nuclear capabilities. There is evidence that the race has accelerated from reports published by the satellite imaging data from British and Colorado sources. Michael Evans, a defence journalist, wrote in the Times London (29-11-1999) that Kashmir situation nearly led to a nuclear clash. Weapons are more in readiness of deployment than before the Kargil episode. Has power struggle between the two taken a new dimension ? We will dedicate this chapter to the present state of nuclear arms, its development and future with particular focus on its impact on Kashmir. Conventions on disarmament have not been effective in enforcing the non-proliferation and testing of weapons treaties in the years of deliberations.

Having led you through groping in dark alleys of tragedy in making, there is a glimmer of light. Some optimism has emanated from the meeting of the five big powers in New York on future of Nuclear Weapons. On the 21st May, 2000, a landmark resolution was passed that nuclear weapons would be abolished from the face of Earth. In this the USA, Russia, UK, France, and China signed up to an unequivocal undertaking to complete elimination of nuclear arsenal. The resolution was passed with 187 countries having signed up to the treaty of Non-proliferation. Five years back this agreement would have been unthinkable.

The question remains how to apply this optimism to the dangers of nuclear proliferation between India and Pakistan. The only blemish to this utopian vision is the American Theatre Missile defence (TMD) policy. If there is going to be a nuclear exchange it will be over Kashmir. The Dhaka declaration issued by the conference attended by 150 activists from 14 countries of Asia and the USA noted that nuclearization has escalated mutual suspicion and hostility between India and Pakistan. It has underpinned communal, militarist, authoritarian and centralising political tendencies within the two countries. The rapidly worsening security environment cannot be redressed by standard confidence building measures. Conference held on the February 18-29, 2000 called for an immediate freezing and dismantling of nuclear arms between the two feuding countries. Once there is an air burst explosion, it will cross all borders, devastating all countries in the region of South Asia and beyond !

	US	Russia	Britain	France	China	Israel	Pakistan	India
Total Stockpile	12070	22500	200	450	400	200	unknown	unknown
Number on Alert	4600	4000	48	100	100+	100+	unknown	unknown
Y2k compliance	doubtful	unlikely	doubtful	unknown	unlikely	unlikely	unknown	unknown

The geography of nuclear warfare, 1999 (New International: 315 Aug. 1999)

1998 figures reveal a staggering amount of a $,1000 billion spent on defence in the world. This inevitably docked investment from structural and social development and progress in science and technology for better living. The proponents of 'More is Worse' hypothesis have roots in organisation theory which stipulates that military behaviour may use nuclear power option for war especially in weak civilian states and new nuclear powers (Sagan). India and Pakistan would be the glaring examples.

In these antics of politics, how would you justify proponents of neo-realist thinking which favours 'More is Better'? This strategy is based on the assumption that to pile up arms to limits, you may deter the enemy and enhance stability. The concept that Japan and Germany should be arming with nuclear weapons as a balancing act, in order to create stability in international security relations, has received support (Mearshaimer). Extending the corollary further it is purported that India and Pakistan may not go to war over Kashmir because nuclear weapons are very expensive to maintain besides being mutually destructive. A view is also held by some nuclear analysts that nuclear weapon capability by India and Pakistan has introduced strategic stability and cautionary factor in their decision making. (Waltz).

The mind boggling dilemma is the unstable triggers, which if we learn from history are replicable even in experienced hands. Swami- krishna Sunderji, former Indian commander-in-chief, alerted nuclear hazard by using the metaphor of six blind men feeling parts of an elephant. Every man would interpret the beast differently. Some observers visiting the region recently compared notes and said Pakistan nuclear facility is completely in the hands of army and organisational theory norms stipulate that a finger on the trigger may be more predictable, while as facilities in India are controlled by politicians and likely to run the risk of political vagaries. There are others who believe that it is the display of organisational behaviour and inflexible routine by the military which may subject the ill fated subcontinent to accidental or deliberate push on that nuclear button. This argument is supported by recent missile deployment along border areas. As already alluded there are blemishes in the truimphalism of nuclear free utopia. The recent declared policy of USA to continue Theatre Missile Defence System (TMD) or son of star wars program and escalating conflict in Kashmir cast a dark shadow.

The USA are not only the undisputed superpower but have become a focus of attention as role models for other aspiring superpowers like China, France and Russia. There are under currents of a race for supermacy. Europe wants to invest in a matching Missile Defence capability. The American array of smart weapons is worth taking a look at. Apart from Tomahawk missiles, Earthquake bombs which burrow deep inside bunkers and explode to cause earthquake within the silos destroying hidden arsenal and military have been used in Afghanistan. Electromagnetic pulse warheads exploded will disable all communication systems. America's futuristic vision has no bounds. Airborne Lasers (ABL) would use satellite stations outside atmosphere as launching base and destroy missiles being fired from earth still in the boost phase. India and Pakistan have a long way to go to even approach star wars technology.

Directed energy weapons could only be deflected by clouds. Unmanned aircraft carrying chemical oxygen laser weapons (COIL) can wander in circles undetectable even by sophisticated radar, find targets on earth and destroy them. In response to these developments the Russian president Valadimir Putin has declared a pro-nuclear defence policy. In our topic under inquiry we will attempt to scrutinise how if any implications of this nuclear scenario will impact on Kashmir. The USA security umbrella should have been impenetrable with no threats to its own borders. That did not eliminate the possible attack on its citizens and allied countries in other parts of the world. September 11 attacks on America blitzered the world. It is natural, the US hegemony and extensive power will bestir an asymmetric war. Attacks on Beirut marines in 1983, World Trade Centre in 1993, embassies in Nairobi and Dar-es-Salam in 1998 and more notably the huge losses suffered in Saudi Khobar Towers in 1996 and recent attack on U S -Cole warship in Aden killing 17 and injuring 40 men are reminders of this legacy.

Kashmir uprising has been allegedly linked to shifting bases of groups involved with rebellion against America. Kashmiri groups, political or militant insurgents, have denied any connection with such organisations or any part in anti-western asymmetric wars. They have declared their focussed goal for liberation of the people of Kashmir. It may be that Gulbadin or Usama-bin-Ladin declare their support for Kashmiris, or even send volunteers to fight alongside militants in Kashmir. That in itself would not implicate insurgents in Kashmir to be a part of the Islamic threat as perceived by the West. The vioce which surface from dessident groups, endorsed by their Political wings like Huriyat, JKLF, or JKPDM and others, den any links with terrorist based in middle East or elsewhere in the world. As a significant corollary the ruling Peoples Democratic Party have not made that connection.

It is a rare exposition in world politics to bring the seminal issues of the conflict in Kashmir to surface and offer advise or a plausible remedy. How many political observers have heard Kashmir mentioned, without having been swamped by issues of hostility between India and Pakistan roped in. No one has ever heard of conflict between Southern Ireland and Great Britain. Instead it is a conflict between republicans and the unionists of Northern Island itself. Kashmir dispute in the eyes of the world has no people content. In other words, if Pakistan vanished from the scene, the conflict is de facto successfully consummated.

Egocentric images peculiar to South Asian social fabric flare up hostility. It was at the very peak of post Kargil tension that the defence minister of India declared first strike nuclear option and flexible response attack if Pakistan army made any gains in war. Whatever the jingoistic attractions may be, both countries have to understand that national security needs are interdependent and self referenced security policy may be counter-productive (Buzan). It is arguably compromising their own security. In the present political climate it is unlikely that India and Pakistan will co-operate in nuclear disarmament. This becomes more difficult with escalating border clashes. There are other factors at play which neo-realists give credence to, including, lack of trust, balance of power and security. India's weapons are plutonium based, with a stockpile of fissile material enough for about 50 warheads. India tested a device in 1974 with likely help from Canadian nuclear reactor technology. Pakistan on the other hand has a single Uranium based fission weapon with capability to produce 12 devices. Both countries have capacity to produce free fall bombs and warheads for medium range ballistic missiles. In the event of a war, when the ruckus is over, there will be no win-win scenes of a civilisation except like the final judgement, a montage of desolation.

Mr Clinton and Mr Putin declared that 68 tons of plutonium from the USA and Russia must be destroyed. (3rd June, 2000). Both powers have breached the 1972 Anti-ballistic Missile (ABM) and non-proliferation treaties. It is important to exhort India and Pakistan that the USA is seeking to change the ABM treaty (Albright: 24th April, 2000; NY) to reflect New Threats from 3rd world countries outside the strategic regime. It is worth noting that she did not mention the so called 'Rogue Nations', a concept now changing with closer ties with Iran and North Korea. Iraq and Libya still remain the excuse for American concern. On a bright note there is a unified campaign from world states (182 signatories of 1970 Treaty) to restrain India, Pakistan and Israel, countries with lex talionis political doctrine and live conflicts.

As a result the New Agenda Coalition (NAC) was formed by a group of Neutral States led by South Africa, Ireland, Brazil, Mexico, Sweden, Egypt and Newzealand to press for further action and ask the New Nuclear states to act responsibly. Kashmir has featured in all discussions. NAC determined that conflicts must be solved if any progress is made in reducing nuclear arsenal. Ending the topic on a sombre note, I can only quote Tom McDonald from the British American Security Information Council who said "Nuclear war is actually more thinkable today than in the past decade following the nuclear tests and building ups by India and Pakistan"

Terrorism and Kashmir

Kashmir dispute has been sidelined in western politics in the mistaken belief that influx of terrorism dominates political dissent in the state. In his book The Goat Justine Hardy while describing the luxury of Pashmina or Cashmere shawls, quotes a New Yorker as saying, " You are not buying Pashmina from Kashmir and helping the terrorists. Are you a Muslim or something ?" In an attempt to critique that perception using empirical and normative experience, terrorism by definition is a state of fear and submission so produced in a sense of an abhorrent behaviour at all levels of politics. There are however questions on who will decide are the actors in this process?

In reliance on the definition of terrorism, how would one assess the degree of fear inducted when dead bodies are seen on the doorsteps of relatives ? In politics, terrorism has been used as a key word to malign dissent or justify brute force to defeat rebellion. This practice was highlighted in the debates held by Socrates in the Agora parlays of Athens. Socrates argued that the Political leaders did not derive power from their wisdom but from majority support with little thought to moral question. He was executed for his defiance of the state and became an apologist for rebellious people in future years. Terrorism took birth in the aftermath of the French Revolution. In a manner similar to justice, terrorism must be seen to be done (Coleman). It may be clandestine but its' aims and objectives are deliberately made clearly known. It may be relevant to cite examples of states acting as terrorists in other places with conflicts or wars. History will not forget the terror used by Stalin during his wars against Germany. Soldiers who did not die in action and returned would be shot and killed when they did. In similar ways terror was a weapon used by Hitler in Germany, Pol Pott in Cambodia and it was used by the state in Guatemala in 1954 and Argentina in 1974. Sadam Hussein used chemical weapons to mutilate dissident Kurd population. It is interesting to notice that perpetrators of terrorism express grave concerns about such conduct when it is aimed against them. A glaring example would be condemnation of terrorism by Mr Benjamin Natanyahu, ex-prime minister of Israel, in his book Terrorism How the West can Win. Apart from what impositions he ordered against the Palestinian population in his country, he is known to have personally authorised the assassination of a Palestinian leader living in Amman. In his book he classified terrorism as antagonist of democracy practised by communist totalitarian and Islamic fundamentalist regimes. The duality of values can only be political expediency.

In the western school of thought 'Terrorism' assumes a pre-judged situation, so that violence from these groups that we disagree with very much, is an illegitimate method, ignoring that the state they are using violence against may itself be illegitimate. (Rubenstein). If terrorism involves kidnapping and assassinations, then who can be held to account for custodial killings, Killing western hostages or disappearances in Kashmir (A.I. Index ASA 20/02/99). In Kashmir the state cannot surgically single out its enemy, it inevitably comes down hard on people and adopt military tactics in peacetime. How do partisan terrorists operate to make the state ungovernable ? It is a subject worth reflection. Rubsenstein maintains that they galvanise support from an already existing nationalist movement, otherwise they would not exist. They draw substance from public feeling and need to be politically motivated. Examples given include IRA and PLO. Their struggles have a spiritual content and the number of intrepid youth plunging into death in suicidal attacks is ever increasing.

The extent and mode of operation terrorist non-state groups practice throws open a debate about the kinds of terrorism, and the driving forces behind their goals. In our inquiry we will confine ourselves to political terrorism as opposed to drug Mafia gangs, etc. Political dissent in Kashmir has been tarnished with the image of terrorism and readily subsumed by the west to slot into their own doctrines. Militants in Kashmir predicate that inducing terror is verboten in their oath of commission. The unilateral ceasefire declared by HM (Hizbul Mujahidin) militant

Chapter ◀12▶

Notes on Paradigms:
Antecedent Factors

In any form of government some basic norms are essential to be universally accepted. A set of rules will have to be drawn up to formalise relationships between all parties and the people of Kashmir. The governing practice would have to declare in a statement form, the political ideals like 'Peace in the region' or joint tourism tactics, or free flow of passport holding citizens of the subcontinent, etc. A set of rules would have to come on board to enshrine a bill of rights safeguarding the freedom of people (Eazar 1985) and interests of India and Pakistan. Efforts to bring the two warring rivals together will take myriad forms. In Kashmir, ideas forming the basis of a credible government will need to straddle between theory and practice to earn legitimacy.

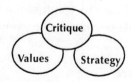

' World view 'or critique of the existing order; on that a model for a better society would have to be constructed

Economic co-operation is avidly accepted but when it comes to a political union the vying powers will shy away, the sovereignty issues and politics encircling that become a heresy. Kashmir allowed to prosper and given a kind of identity based on modernity where development takes a priority, would culminate into a progressive state ensuring equitable distribution of resources. As a part of the subcontinent, the nascent state would share the vagaries of corruption, as well as quixotic ideals of a super-continent. It may however be possible to install honest bureaucratic channels which override the concerns of the temporary appointment of or elected politicians of any nationality.

Inevitability for Peace: There is an implicit inevitability for a resolution of Kashmir dispute. How can India afford hostility on all its borders and a military impasse over perpetual violent insurrection in the state that it controls? How can anyone wish away the realities of the situation ? How can Pakistan afford to be duelling with a power four times its size for all times to come and still make any attempt at progress ? How can you predict what the people of Kashmir would do and in which ways react if one of the two big powers controlling their lives were to collapse or be defeated in a war ? Would they be expected to remain in perpetual obeisance to the winner, or die for the country whose side they belong now ? An adroit observer of hard core politics will find it difficult to foretell. There is increasing awareness of loss of life on a daily basis from all three sides, that people will not reconcile and settle for this destructive low intensity war. Loss of life will bring to a head the emotions and increasing concern about the futility of ending so many precious lives. Whatever the culture of war dictates, human life is not implicitly dispensable. How long can you fuel the war with martyrs being thrown in to the flames raging the conflict.

Complex Nature

Comparison drawn with contemporary conflicts makes Kashmir stand out in a peerless category. There are three legitimate parties in Kashmir, and they are all fighting for the same territory. In

East Timor, Portuguese were not a party in contention apart from moral support and empathy for the freedom seeking people.

It was East Timories against Indonesia. Similarly in Kosovo or Palestine, there are only two communities in conflict. It gives the Kashmir dispute a special place in international politics. Kashmir is the only hot spot which is the longest running dispute with three parties spilling blood in its streets and nuclear weapons being flashed at each other. In the subcontinent the milieu of terror, insecurity and political anarchy is pervasive in all cities and villages. Violence has bred hardcore nationalist diatribe overcoming moderate liberalist thinking. It is widely believed that an opportunity was lost during the period of decolonisation to forestall all possible disputes. At that time solutions could be imposed and lines of statehood drawn. From then on the dispute was portrayed in different ways and tied inextyicably into the international security dynamic.

Cold war period saw the world distancing from Kashmir with preoccupation elsewhere. The concept related to security issues has put a new complexion on Kashmir. Major threat it has been argued comes from the so called Green Islamic Menace and not so much from Red Russian Revanchism (Mortimer 1992). Kashmir has been caught in the middle of this political web and indigenous freedom struggle identified with international extremist movement, further complicating the conflict. The French philosopher/ academic Jacques Derrida (1930-) challenged the perception of Islamic cultural identity in terms of fundamentalism. In response to this threat the western powers have adopted containment policies which may have relevance to Kashmir. First one is to avoid getting involved in conflicts with Islamic peril and the second is to discourage self-determination and creation of new states. Civilians were crushed ruthlessly in Chechnya and Kosovo. The West in line with their policy opposed independence for both countries, even though NATO intervened in Kosovo in order to undermine Serbian defiance. Chechnyan devastation in full view of the world made little impact.

For India, Kashmir has intrinsic flaws like ethnic divisions and demographic distribution of a Muslim majority population which may cause impediment to the peace process in presaging an untoward outcome of a plebiscite. Celebrating the Buddhist tradition Dalai Lama, the Tibetan leader, said 'boundaries are not important' (Radio-4 December, 1999). He wants China to have control of Tibetan economy and offer Tibetans a local autonomous rule. It follows therefore borders become hard with hard adversarial politics. The normative theorists will accept a compromised solution for Kashmir, notwithstanding the empirical research revealing a high intensity civil war with loss of lives on a daily basis accompanied by destruction of the infrastructure and habitat. Legally it may be an unlikely prospect to assign absolute sovereignty of Kashmir to India or Pakistan. If Kashmir is decreed not to be a part of India or Pakistan, then by implication, International laws have been broken by the mere presence of armed forces from both countries. A nation state is protected from violations of its borders. This law was reinforced by the UN General Assembly resolution 2131, 1965.

In order to get an agreement from all parties, the following concerns would have to be met.

Security and Defence

In application of norms of empiricism in the highly charged radical politics of India and Pakistan, security takes a prime position. It may be argued that recent global threats to security supersede the ethno-centric concerns of core values like freedom of individuals or states. In my view South Asian subcontinent will need safeguards against occult forces of the corporate world and exploitation of its huge populous from being subsumed, politically and economically. It is only if and when political wisdom prevails that credence may be given to the idea of a self preserving United Asia. Indian and Pakistani military would have to disengage along all their borders, gradually and in line with progress made on the political front. It may be possible that both armies are seen as a friendly force, interacting with each other and the people. It is common knowledge that the two nuclear powers will abandon the expensive nuclear arsenal as and when the Kashmir dispute has been amicably resolved. Further along in chapter 14, I will reiterate the importance of an Asian Military Alliance. That may only be a dream! But it is worth a serious thought any time

Sovereignty over Territory

Both countries it is hoped will prepare themselves in loosening up political control over some of the territory and aim for a devolved state, merger of the two parts of Kashmir and a joint administrative control. The expectation would be that a decade or so of interim rule may alter the political environment and a final solution becomes a reality. In order to maintain sovereignty it is apparent all faces of power will need to be used in Kashmir in order to achieve the desired outcome of a compliant society. This includes the radical face of power or 'Thought Control'. This change will need to sway mindset towards a gunfree culture of a progressive society. The liberalist would like civic loyalties in contrast with the conservative notion of organic unity which in case of Kashmir may be difficult to achieve.

In giving the people a fair deal, there are normative concerns about feelings of being treated as inhabitants of property claimed to be owned by others. Property and ownership of property in philosophical terms is theft because no one has eternal right to property, especially so where mother Earth is concerned. The dangers are that it is these material assets and furtive deals in occupation of lands which lead to tyranny, a concept set out by Pierre Joseph Proudhan, a French anarchist philosopher (1842) and has resonance in today's political culture of Kashmir. In some respects Palestine also is in sufferance for land

Economic Benefits over Political Culture

As a part of peace package, measures would need to be put in place to ensure that integrated economic system is employed so that India, Pakistan and Kashmir improve on their mutual economical benefits. Kashmir employed as an asset may offer an export orientated industry and tourism which would be a spur for economic growth for both India and Pakistan (Siraj). In the event that India and Pakistan develop strong economic relations, it will make adversarial confrontation difficult. In 1625 Emric Cru-ce advocated free trade as a means of promoting peace; Four centuries later there seems to be an opportunity to draw upon the wisdom in that saying.

Paradigm Shift.

India, Pakistan and the world will need to have confidence that the phased and possibly long drawn peace process in Kashmir will be effective and that when a settlement is in sight, there would need to be irrevocable covenants in a written treaty that no one will back out from. Taking a lesson from the hypothetical concept of the 'prisoner's dilemma' incumbent politicians will find themselves behind bars for guilt and wrongfully failing to collaborate. They could only achieve freedom without having to rat on others in similar situations. The North (Western World) plays the part of the prison governor in this metaphor, presumably because they want to keep both countries under control. In real world and the finality of events dictates that the mindset has to change into a paradigm shift from use of army and physical force to economic race based on peace in the region by both India and Pakistan. Political activists in Kashmir on their part may also need to streamline their struggle, taking a lesson from Lenin's formation of pragmatist Bolshevik type vanguard party which in the main relied upon expediency in preference to perpetual culture of violence.

State in Transition

> There is perpetual and restless desire for power; That ceaseth only in death:
> (Thomas Hobbes 1588-1679)

All hostilities have a causal effect and originate from common elements at play. This culture of bitterness will not only cease in Kashmir but in all parts of the subcontinent. It is believed that violence in Northeast India, Punjab, Karachi or Kashmir are inter-related. Terrorist groups and partisan insurgents will not be able to operate or get logistic support if all countries in the region have a built in understanding of mutual respect in their relations. It stands to reason that a treaty will only come into effect if a deal is struck on Kashmir, even to the extent of making it a virtual state.

Kashmir may be a protectorate which is being transformed into a polity in future days with consideration of the total interests of all parties in contention. The portfolios of defence, foreign affairs and communication could have close collaboration between India, Pakistan and the State government. It may be that a consensual framework is evolved in future which enables a participation by all three parties. In brief, Kashmir could be held as a 'state in transition' within the framework of a paradigm, as will be discussed further on in the book. The essence of a move taken in this way could be construed as a cooling off period and an essential ingredient of a stepping stone provided to start the peace process without compromising the status quo and legitimacy of India and Pakistan inside the positions they now hold.

Free and Fast Communications

What hopes of a peace accord can we expect, if there is an exceptional dialogue held reluctantly between India and Pakistan for propaganda purposes only and interspersed within invective quibbling, which in the event is soaked up eagerly by hungry media ? Cold war came to an end without a mishap because hot lines were established between top executives of super powers, reinforced with fibre-optic cables laid across the Atlantic ocean. Communications are as important to achieve peace as for preventing war. More often it is communication failure which can trigger wars. One such example would be the Gulf war. Sadam Hussain misconstrued the nod of consent he received from the American ambassador saying 'Yes' to invasion of Kuwait which lead up to the eventual devastation of Iraq. The inadvertent murder of the heir to Austrian throne in Sarajevo on 28th June, 1914, set off the World War One, even allowing for other tensions which existed prior to that incident. The more recent incident of USA launching the Black Brunt Mark 12 sounding rocket from Norway (January 1995) almost started super power war. It was a civilian satellite launch. The Russians were not informed. Their radars registered electro-magnetic signals coming from a ballistic missile loaded submarine. The whole war machinery was alerted by Russia. A nuclear response was activated. When someone sought information and came to know about the true nature of the signals a nuclear war was averted. India and Pakistan do not trust each other. Even a telephone call may not be enough to avert a crisis if a false alarm is initiated by error or ingenuous handling. Communication at all levels from NGO's to the top executives and every-day in my view is the bedrock of success of any peace process in Kashmir. In the end it will be the logic of rationality and teleological concerns which will prevail.

Thinking Globally

Our prison is the world of our perceptions (Plato).

Asians have their own adage to explain the principal put forth by Plato. They call it the 'Toad's life' - toad, living in a pond will perceive the retaining walls as the horizon and the water around an ocean. It may be that parochial attitude pervasive in South Asian Society Constricts ways and means of a resolution. Kashmir from ancient times was at the crossroads of regional globalisation.

There was regular traffic of cultural and social artefacts across the daunting Himalayan peaks and Pamir range from Central Asia, Mongolia and Tibet. Passes were permeable all through summer months. British holiday makers often came across travelling merchants who sold tea (usually like a brick), exotic silk garments, embroidered sheets, printed cotton from Russia and strange barbaric jewellery (Macmillan). The trade was taking place between all countries in the region. Kashmir ended up being a manufacturing hub for cashmere shawls and garments. No one had any thoughts about carrying passports or paying import duties or setting tariffs. It was one big happy bazaar what would now be called globalisation. Kashmir has a historical background to support its free market trading tradition. I remember the days in early forties, when the long robed and bearded merchants from Central Asia descended into the capital city of Kashmir with their beautiful merchandise. They were accommodated in Iddgah Sarais (Inns). I recall the most delectable recipe for lamb they cooked. Transactions were structured on the basis of barter system. They went back across the mountain passes loaded with merchandise from Kashmir.

If we consider the Earth to be an organism, which exhibits signs of self regulation, than Kashmir is a small component of the same living system or call it the Gaia.

" I shall sing of Gaia, Universal mother, firmly founded, the oldest of Divinities " Homer.

Thinking globally on Kashmir quickly changes our perception of the dispute. If the state is a microcosm of universal political system and has history of a tradition of global traffic through trade and tourism, then why not create a niche for it in the world's open Bazaar. Globalisation is unravelling state sovereignty. The Gaia Atlas of Future Worlds (1990) presents the concepts of dynamic peace and planetary citizenship. India and Pakistan would have to abandon their constricted parochial vision and broaden their attitude in line with the changes taking place in the international community. There is a saying that 'Politics is local, but increasingly all local politics has global consequences' (Anan).

Kashmir is a constituent of the global village and shares values stemming from ideals of macro-perspective that views the whole world as an integrated and inter-dependent whole. Borders like the line of control in Kashmir will become irrelevant. The pervasive strands of global politics allowed to permeate through the borders of unified polity will help to soften attitudes and bring issues of mutual benefit like structural integration, industrial growth, network of markets and communications closer. In a globalised polity, Kashmir may absorb larger share of the world's prosperity, help from the United Nations aid agencies and global charities. Cruc'e advocated 'Free Trade to promote Peace'. The axiom can be made to work for Kashmir. The exotic scenery, golf courses and Himalayan peaks may attract multinational companies to set up in Kashmir and utilise the talented local labour force, well known for their hands on skills. Albeit the downside of open market system leading to depredation and social suffering it brings may be a price people are prepared to pay and has to be born in mind. Environment and health issues will home in on an already devastated population. Kashmir once considered a spa, an expanse of a health farm, is now a composite of polluted cities and abraded rural habitat.

On the political front, the real prospect of evading crisis are regressive in the face of centrifugal pressures from within and upsurge of regional tensions. All these factors remain live in the political culture of Kashmir while violence in the streets perpetuates unbridled degradation. Let us revel in our indulgence and send all the forces and militants on a holiday! Would sovereignty be threatened ? How long and how far would globalisation take control and make the return of the gunmen unwelcome. Would people be able to resist the change ? The view to ponder is that, in the face of the rapid and pervasive nature of international politics, would the hard boiled proponents of statehood have lost their grip, even before the guns arrive back on scene. Globalisation makes inroads in powerful ways. What are its impacts on the political culture of Kashmir?

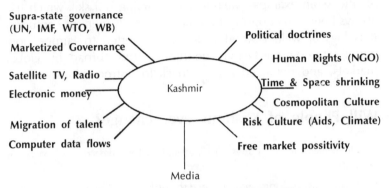

Kashmir as a part of Global village

It is argued that realist's vision of state power is waning at the same rate as societies of the world connect through technology. India and Pakistan are at the forefront of technology and India has one of the leading IT industrial bases of the world. How can they escape the sequel replete with blatant transformation? Is it ever possible for India or Pakistan to shut off their country to the rest of the world, reverse the process of globalisation and claim every internal matter for them is not international business or that they can internalise disputes like Kashmir as and when they feel is expedient for them?

Translated into today's reality kashmir it would work on lines of a duty free offshore paradise where holidays would be combined with shopping of a life time. Present day globalisation is less open than existed in old times (Hirst & Thompson 1996). Back in those days there was no protectionism, no WTO tariffs and restraints. Politics and language flowed across freely. A nudge must wake us up to the realities of globalisation with a strong presence of the world system theory over-shadowing the liberalist traditions. The danger is that elements of globalisation creates international capitalism and widens class divide with exploitation of labour and raw materials. Persistence of cyclical political upheavals left Kashmiris no room to develop expertise. The risk of exploitation of proletariat and indigenous raw material became reality. As an example, walnut wood carving is a skill which has always been a monopoly of the Kashmiri craftsmen for centuries. It is logs of walnut wood which get exported to Europe now (Siraj). State interests may be represented abroad by global markets, and not need a piggy back for introductions.

Will People of Kashmir ever change?

Tormented souls ' If it does not kill them, it makes them stronger ' (Nietzsche 1844-90).

Kashmir has a long way to go to universal liberal democracy because its people have hurdles to cross in overturning sanctions on their subjectivity. Fukuyama, it may be argued, has ignored flaws in his vision, like Kashmir and Palestine. Human beings have a tendency to change and adopt to conditions of environment. Disregarding the traditions of the Darwinian evolution which has a long-life span, we will concern ourselves with short term outcome of eventful politics in Kashmir. Karl Marx believed that every man has needs and has power which he will use to satisfy those needs. Man is corporeal, living, real in body and spirit, sensuous, and objective, a being, and not merely a disembodied mind. People of Kashmir do not exist simply because they can think loud and they may not be able to control tendencies and impulses that seek fulfilment in a variety of needs like eating, sex, jobs, social companionship, variety in activity apart from political freedom. Force used to restrain this process of change is not conceivable.

Taking a lesson from history we know that the British used tactics to repress insurrection, like divide and rule, play the race card, actively succour the weaker groups to defeat the stronger forces, throw spanner in the works by killing a priest or beheading a cow in the midst of fanatic Hindus, penalise activists and reward collaborators, use local renegade forces to kill their own people and so on. All these methods have been employed in Kashmir various times. Their copy-cat nature and familiar tones of history amazingly become ineffective to a common man living in a far flung village so much aware of the politics which surrounds him. It may be that these policies worked for a time in Kashmir, and calm was seen as peace.

Events leading up until the liberation of India from the British reveal, what was happening inside the minds of Indian freedom fighters was not apparent to the incumbent ruling administration and may have a resemblance to the perceptions of the common man in Kashmir. The dynamism of change pulsated in all human forms creating new concepts. In the years bygone the uprising in Kashmir has aped the revolt of its mother country, using that experience as a starting point nevertheless spurred on a movement in forward direction. Let me explain the phenomenon of why old concepts stop making room for new ideology by using the metaphor of the owl from Hegel's teachings. The owl takes flight when the day is over and finds another perch in far away place. The owl never flies backwards. The day has gone, the doctrines are petering out, all old theories are loosing their impact. Politics likewise moves on. The owl makes progress by finding another perch. It is therefore imperative that the navigating forces change direction if the tide of untamed waves have to be neutralised. The message will in simple words be that as time goes on, posterity will gain credence from the experiences of elders and who knows the flames of dissent and rebellion may take a new direction even more difficult to contain. It may as a consequence be inferred that people of Kashmir have already changed and will go on changing at a faster speed now than ever before.

The impact of global politics is making inroads into the minds of people through all forms of communication systems. Kashnet, a discussion forum on the Internet, was started in Colorado ten years back and has a membership of over 200. It is accessed by major political parties and individuals involved in Kashmir politics, Pakistan and Indian government agencies and NGO groups (kashmir-global-network-owner@yahoogroups.com). Criticisms and membership applications are received by ajazsiraj@yahoo.com or kashnet@indra.com. Newspapers and Human Rights Organisations from the subcontinent including

Kashmir are the mainstay of transfer of information in either direction. It is not hard to understand why people in Kashmir have a vertical rise in the pace of development in acquisition of knowledge about world politics and awareness about how it could influence their struggle for a future. It is an amazing revelation to have been told that a Technology park has come to be a physical reality in Kashmir and people are flocking in to join in the spectre.

An anecdote from my recent visit to a remote village (Duru Kashmir) will make the point. I thought the Western technology-Duru interface would be an infinity ! To my amazement, I was introduced to a computer centre. "I own this school. I teach young students software and window applications. Unfortunately they only pay me in kind, like a bag of walnuts!" My local contact tells me. They can identify themselves with the rest of the people of the world and wonder why they do not enjoy the same rights as individuals like everyone else. It follows implicitly that to colonise any people now would be an uphill task for any new player in this politics. Globalised information discourse creates a mindset that structures understanding and behaviour implicit in rights to the general will. (Rousseau 1712-78).

We must offer alternatives even if that means negative Freedom* or laissezaler polity.

In order to dispel darkness and seek common good, we will take three steps back and make room for Peace.

In circumstances where peremptory access is provided to people to plausible alternatives to the way they live, we as workers for peace have to sum up the desire to drive us to

---

* Negative Freedom implying non-interference by the government in the decision making as long as they do not interfere with Freedom of others except to maintain peace.. Negative Freedom will in time progress to a democratic system placed in public sphere.

promote the ways and means to make the possible options easily understood and assist to implement them judiciously. The idea of horizontal thinking allows room for extending our imagination.

This alone has to be feared, the closed mind,
The sleeping imagination, The death of the spirit. (Plato)

Framework for Paradigmatic Models:
Peace in Kashmir

The template for each paradigm could be shaped in the following manner. It is important to note that the paradigms are not explanations of the views expressed by me but a suggested interpretation as viewed by the world. Even in a dominant paradigm we cannot forbid future or imminent intellectual critique and change its structure. Paradigm by its character is a fixed arrangement of a set of forms, containing essentially the same element, for us 'Peace'. These include:

Assumptions: Stereotyped hostile imagery: Civilian space for reconciliation.

The Blueprint: A sketch of the mechanics in the construction of the model.

Functional Strategy: The working patterns, suitable and logical.

Advantages: Benefits to India, Pakistan or people of Kashmir.

Feasibility: Will it work ? Will it last ? Will it be acceptable ?

Future: Prospects for durable peace and progress in South Asia.

Models for solutions are suggested so they can be worked upon or used as sketches for the architects building bridges for peace. Moderates from all three parties, it is hoped, will be the important players at the core of the peace process. There will be arguments, debates, exchange of rhetoric and evidence as maps and documents. I am also sure there are other ways of resolving the conflict that I have not touched upon, nevertheless even to list possibilities may work as a nudge in the direction of an amity and reconciliation.

Paradigms

Third Party intervention: Arbitration, United Nations; Negotiations

Status in quo: Line of Control converted to international borders; Political artefacts (Simla).

Conjoint Rule: Three commissioners; Power sharing executive; Partial Autonomy; Shared sovereignty; Pooled sovereignty.

Asian Parliament: South Asian Parliament in Kashmir and Military Alliance (AMA)

Independence.   Self Determination; Modified Dixon Plan.

Emulate existing political models in other disputed regions of the world: Comparative Peace Process. Trusteeship/Mandated territory/Protectorate status

Third Party Intervention

India is one among the three parties who oppose mediation and intervention system applicable to Kashmir. Albeit India being a liberal democracy with increasing epistemic content in population may be forced to see the benefits of this approach used with success in other conflicts of the world. The third party facilitators provide theoretical inputs which help participants with conceptual tools for analysis, distance from hostility and converge their focus on blind spots and positive signals. World community has over the past fifty years tried to offer mediation to facilitate dialogue. The normative perceptions which prevail in the subcontinent make a strong case for salience of renewed attempts at intervention diplomacy. Words of philosophical artefacts may offer guidance and wisdom in the choice of the path we take. Michael de Montaigne in 16th century equates dogmatism with ignorance. If a mediator does become a reality in that case the whole complexion of the conflict will change. The parties will have already come half way up the road to peace process and accepted in unison some of the essential ingredients of the dispute, including the historical background, the legal facts, ethical norms and emphasis on the welfare of the people and not territory.

It is just possible that a way is found which did not entail holding a plebiscite and yet would have universal acceptance. It may be argued by apologists for India's stand on Kashmir that bringing a credible mediator would give India the best chance of a tenable package. It was mediation which persuaded PLO in the end to accept limitations in their demands. PLO in open forums spurned outright some of these restrictions. In reliance on the experience of Oslo Track II mediation, Indian side would take comfort from the position of the bargaining scale, very much like Israel and achieve certain objectives wrapped in peace.

In mediation Adam's model of hard and soft style Tract II procedures may be used. There is evidence that an agreement between the USA and Russia is now possible on their policy on Kashmir and if both stepped in to support the mediation effort, with offer of incentives and a measure of concerted pressure applied, it could make foreseeable peace possible.

Track II mediation attempts over Kashmir have already been attempted, they did not move forward because the people involved in the process did not have support from the executives in governments. In Oslo the academics had direct lines of communication with their respective governments. In preparation for mediation, experts bring all common ground between disputants together and float various permutation within options available.

It is possible that hard line options now adopted are discouraged as temporising obstacle. It would be expedient to support the view that an atmosphere is created for the mediation to succeed. It may not be enough to repeat the confidence building gestures made in the past, because they have already lived their day Instead new ground breaking notable offers which make a difference have to be employed. It may for example be valid for India to invite a diplomat from Pakistan to visit parts of Kashmir administered by them and address a conference on peace. It is very unlikely he will use the opportunity to spew diatribe to promote violence. It may bring confidence in the peace process on all sides. The offer may in theory be reciprocated by Pakistan. The visits could be repeated in order to encourage animated interaction with civil society and political activists on both sides of the divide. We may say that the Lahore visit of Mr Vajpayee was a step forward. The truth is that it was a great move towards peace. Why was it then waylaid? Back to the pavilion and good old harangue of abuse and hostility. This is where a third party mediation could have interceded. Having made an inch of progress, another inch would be spurred in forward direction by capable handling of the mediation teams.

Renaissance of United Nations Role

It is well known that United Nations had constraints in its mandate to implement solutions in Kashmir, notwithstanding all the resolutions passed and UNCIP delegations who worked so hard in the subcontinent to bring a lasting peace and failed. It is argued that the political climate of the world has changed and the United Nations is in a better position now to take up the issue than it was at the peak of the cold war. The following reasons are worth a mention:

The United Nations Security Council can expect consensus decision making in most cases, with the end of cold war. Russia is not in the same position today as it was in 1948 when as a super-power it played an obstructive role in security council if only to defy the actions of the adversarial West. Invasion of Afghanistan by the USSR was different. Those days, if America had not provided the stinger missiles to Afghan fighters, Russia would be pounding over Afghan position today like they are doing in the Caucasus and Osama bin Laden would not have spawned Al-Queda from that country. The political climate has changed. Now Russia has a furtive acquiescence from NATO for its role in Chechnya.

The United Nations presiding over sovereign nations, has a mandate as stipulated in Article 1 (2) of its charter that it will protect Human Rights and self-determination and be involved with settlement of disputes. The UN in its infancy then, now has the capacity to initiate collective measures essential for the maintenance of peace in the new political climate. (Russet). Taking a clue from deductive logic, India and Pakistan after more than half a century of fierce battles fought, are ready for peace now, a view shared by all liberalist moderates in the region.

The United Nations in the last fifty years has grown out of its infancy and is stronger with its power exercised through its subordinate agencies and affiliate organisations.. It would be possible to link development projects to real peace efforts. The United Nations has a vested interest to see an end to this longest running unfinished business languishing for so long. The UN observers in Kashmir are a costly burden and serve no purpose. IMF an affiliate organisation through a unified opprobrium warned Jakarta that aid would be suspended if the killings in Dilli did not stop. That posture of collective effort gave a big boost to the UN resolution No. 1264 and multinational forces were allowed in East Timor to supervise the elections and assist in comparatively peaceful transition to independence. The United Nations would have to shake off its apathy towards Kashmir and blow the dust away from the pending file of the most virulent and dangerous dispute of the world. Mr Kofi Annan has visited other conflict regions of the world. Is South Asia not important enough? Or dangerous enough? Or is Kashmir not considered in the list of major conflicts with the burden of six killings a day for over a decade to its credit? Is the United Nations waiting for a pageantry of nuclear explosions, before it will condescend to act? Is it true that India and Pakistan are not paying enough towards the organisation, or sending enough soldiers to help the United Nations in peace making and peace keeping efforts in other conflict regions of the world, to be entitled for help in their own conflicts ravaging their countries?

Is the United Nations sold out to its supreme hierarchy? Should the poor nations still continue to owe allegiance and support or are they used as numbers to emphasise North-South divide? The United Nations nominal observers housed in comfortable accommodation in Kashmir have almost no role to play. They do not even report the daily killings along the line of control or make known the intelligence they get about the events of wars fought in the streets of Kashmir under their observations. India and Pakistan accuse each other of shelling the civilians living in border areas and never investigated or adjudicated by the observers. What function do they perform is a good question to ask.

Negotiations

" We may ask why direct action? Isn't negotiation a better path? Indeed, call for negotiations is the purpose of direct action. It seeks so to dramatise the issue that it can no longer be ignored" (Martin Luther King).

In a successful negotiation, the premise must be that everyone wins. The objective should be agreement and not victory. Negotiation is an integral part of everyday life. People exchange ideas with the intention of changing relationships, remove misunderstanding, and whenever they confer for agreement they are negotiating. India and Pakistan have met at different times and based the substance of their dialogue on past treaties. Having carried the logic to its insane end , agreed to disagree and meet again. Each time a show of powerful personalities and pedantic discourse carried the day to a win-lose bargaining situation. In order to change direction and put on tract integrative negotiations, parties in dispute, including the people of the state should choose their own experts with positive exclusion of obdurate and short tempered politicians. The job will still be a challenge. Assuming structural realism has a part to play in conflict management, it is the anarchical system in Kashmir which promotes insecurity and distrust in the masses. The peace making process has to adopt 'conflict managers' approach as ' realists' and be inclusive. It is important to be receptive to bad guys as well as be conciliatory to the demands of victims and respond to all cultures of the society assuming their moral equivalence. The 200,000 Hindus and many thousands of Muslim refugees of Kashmir are suffering in squalid camps and need to be restored back to their homes. It may be relevant to examine issues of dissent by taking a clue from recent history of political struggles in other parts of the world.

The managers from all sides will start from the position of being neutral and see peace as a prime objective and a precondition to future negotiation rather than the negotiating process as pre-condition to peace. India did offer talks with Hisbul Mujahidin. An unprepared and ingenuous attempt at negotiation failed. Electing representatives from Kashmiris may be fraught with difficulties but for negotiations All Party Huriyat Conference (APHC) has been accepted by Pakistan as interlocutor for dialogue. It only requires a nod of approval from India and the process will move forward. Having in place all the ingredients, a systems approach could be developed with eight inter-linked areas of activity including conflict resolution professionals, business community, private citizens, educationists, militants and political activists, religious leaders, politicians and the media, chosen from India, Pakistan and Kashmir. Preparations are essential to put a framework in place before negotiations take place.

The pre-negotiation arena of peace process underpins the foundations of the final outcome (Saunders). Preparing the ground to spawn the process of negotiating for Kashmir, in my view a multitude of options have to be thrashed out in fine detail and a presentation circulated. If we were to skip this phase , we will find ourselves negotiating about identities, fears, suspicions, anger, historical grievances, Kargil war, security concerns, dignity, honour, justice, mutual respect, hegemony and so on. In order therefore to provide a workable framework for negotiations, it is important to achieve an agenda setting climate with positive exclusion of obstructive political issues. Negotiating for peace alone will be for the greater good of advertising their democracy and the benefit of trading partners. Hardliners will be seen on deeper inquiry to be temporising in support of politics of Realism. The instrument of Multi-track Diplomacy is an established method of negotiations and has worked in many other conflict situations. Tract II Nemrana group (Niaz Mallik and others) have already put a lot of effort in making a dialogue possible.

This group could be given help and encouragement to be used for peace building efforts from the grassroots level. Such channels aim to supplement and feed into the official negotiation process (Diamond). In Kashmir the civil society as a whole has been splintered and it may take some searching to find the right people for the systems approach to be used with success. A broad spectrum of the society needs to be pro-actively involved in the way negotiations are progressing. It is important not to draw in famous world personalities because that will be construed as mediation or interventionist, which we all know has been rejected by India. Progress will be made with help from experts and professionals in the field. They maintain a discrete distance from sensitivities and work initially by just clerking the proceedings as they get underway. They help in drawing up the structure of an agenda and try to get the confidence of the parties so they can be relied on to keep official secrecy and discretion during their contact with media. They will gradually play a vital role in steering the proceedings in forward direction and turning crucial corners. It will for example be expected for them to direct discussions on collaborating or integrative (WIN-WIN) modes. On this tract the needs of all parties are taken seriously and considered simultaneously.

It is inevitable that impediments will mar progress, in which case the efforts of the experts will be called upon to redirect discussions towards compromising or accommodating modes. There are other ways the experts can use their finesse and separate image from actual problems or find integrative issues contained in the underlying interests. In tackling Kashmir conflict, the biggest source of failure in negotiations will be to disregard the integrative elements, important to India, Pakistan or Kashmir. Experts will step in to sum up the elements of common interests and encourage exchange of proposals and counter-proposals. It is expected that the initial offers will be extreme and idealistic and focus will have to be directed to alternatives. The intangibles will need remedial measures, like Aspirin for pain. Tension increases, time drags on and fatigue sets in. Negotiations need to be hosted in an open and comfortable venue.

Taking a lesson from the theory of causal relation (Hume 1711-76) past events lead me to believe that the negotiation on Kashmir will become constricted on debate about 'who gets what'? It may be useful to adopt a different route at this stage and to broaden the pie. As an example a limited slice of territory from northern areas or Punjab or Himachal could be brought within the fold of the package. Maps and geographical archetypes would be laid on the table at the same time as going over the dejavo revelations of James Abbot (1847) and Cyril Radcliff (1947) exactly almost a century apart drawing the same boundaries. I will illustrate the principle with a geometrical quiz. (See diagram) Once you learn the solution, it becomes easy to see why our own mental limitations keep our attention focussed within the boundaries. The solution was always there, only we had to seek it. The task in the quiz is to connect nine dots placed within the boundaries of a square with four straight lines without taking your pen off the paper. The correct solution becomes possible only when you extend your line outside the boundaries of dots in the square.

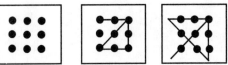

Broaden the Pie

In our assumptions we cannot rule out non-specific compensations like exchange of land elsewhere, water , electricity or just commodities for concessions made in Kashmir. It will emulate the log-rolling exercise common in government departments. In our endeavour to bring life into any of the paradigms considered, our central focus has been the concept of bridging the divergent positions and take on board all options in circulation analysed that satisfy the major interests of all.

Status in quo

" We have to learn to think of in a new way. Remember your humanity and forget the rest " (Bertrand Russell)

Convert LOC into International Border.

The idea of a minimalist approach in dealing with the dispute and expect a fatigue to set in, is simplistic at best and pernicious at worst, if we consider the totality of losses in the region. In the conceptual analysis of the conflict in terms of its common understanding, this solution will set in concrete the very foundations of the conflict. Line of Control (LOC) is perceived as a live volcano. It divides peoples' homes much the same way as other artefacts of wars like the Berlin wall from Russian invasion or the 38th parallel delineating North and South Korea when the Americans dislodged the Japanese from the South and the Russians occupied the North in August 1945. These monuments changed the people in ideology and norms in progress. In Kashmir half a century of isolated lifestyle and juxtaposition of two ideologies, they still show emotions and die for their brothers on the other end of the dividing lines. However there is one outstanding contributing factor, common in all situations. All these lines are drawn like Ghaza and West bank through military occupations and have the intrinsic flaw of standing out as memorials for the extensive injuries inflicted on mankind as the end result of wars and violence.

LOC in Kashmir meanders through some of the highest mountains of the world and is studded with army pickets from both sides. In this terrain soldiers die without a shot being fired. The cost of maintaining these men along this line is not only in human terms but also at an expense of billion of dollars, an inept drain of resources from the coffers of these two poor countries. In the meantime the scenic Himalayan landscape is blemished with smoke bellowing out from the machine guns and the sound reverberating through the snow capped peaks. As collateral damage, the wild life have receded into the jaws of extinction, glaciers have shrunk and avalanches started causing widespread devastation. People of Kashmir will have to carry most of the burden. All along the line they live as servile community, catering to the needs of the resident army. They work as mules, porters, servants, and forced suppliers of their produce. Their life remains on hold and children have been born and brought up in the atmosphere of massive army camps on war alert, surrounding them. In simple deontological terms, you can clearly see the stupidity in supporting such an international border, quite apart from confronting each other like polar beers and feeding the vultures with dead bodies, we are having to redefine the border every time there is an avalanche or a snow drift. Why do we have to defend mountains? After all in the past it was the mountains which defended us!

The National Conference Party in Kashmir supports the idea of freezing the line as international border, as a feasible option. The premise is that India and Pakistan will never relinquish territory already held by them, a paradox to theorise the Mexican stand-off. Defenders of this solution believe that over a period of time these borders will assume international status. Political fatigue will set in and the movement for re-unification will be marginalised. Taking a political slant on this paradigm, is there a hint of discrimination against Kashmir? In current international politics where else have military gains been consolidated into hard borders? Was Sadaam Hussain allowed to draw borders in Kuwait, or Indonesia in East Timore, or Israel in West Bank and

Ghaza? In Kashmir all the factors considered in teleological terms lead us to think and question, whether this kind of international border, if at all possible, be a prelude to lasting peace? Taking a stock of Preventing views on both sides and contextualization of the likely follow on implications, it would stand to scrutiny if such a solution were to be visualised.

Resurrect Past Accords

Shimla Ageement: There is enough substance in the metaphysical analysis of the past agreements to critique and even parody the climate they were set in and their dubious outcome in relation to Kashmir dispute. In some accords items agreed are anachronistic for today's proactive issues. Politics has moved on and open wars have changed their character. Simla agreement signed on July 3rd, 1972, was intended for India and Pakistan to bring an expensive war to an end and ceasefire. The terms of the agreement made an indirect reference to a dialogue on Kashmir, but it was basically about ending Bangladesh war, return of POW's and respecting LOC in Kashmir. India has now been insisting on using Simla as a vehicle for a peace process between the two countries. Simla agreement may be given a sublime status, but unfortunately it is empty in its content and bereft of any specifics about Kashmir. 'Yes', India says we will talk about Kashmir, only let us first take up the issue of Kashmir which Pakistan has occupied. In these deliberations and exchanges, who cares about the lives of people in Kashmir? There are no starting or finishing lines for any dialogue on Kashmir in Simla agreement. Has Simla accord been used more as a means of prevarication and expediency than an instrument for negotiations? A positivist view will offer a ray of hope if discursive arguments are avoided.

Tashkent Accord: The USSR intervention culminated into Tashkent agreement in an effort to end the 1965 war. The declaration was signed in good faith by heads of state from both countries on the 10th January, 1966, affirming that no future wars will be waged. It is rumoured that an agreement was arrived at on Kashmir. Unfortunately that was not to materialise. Kashmir suffered a blow by the sudden death of the Indian Prime Minister Mr Shastri with whom the deal had been struck. The other parts of the agreement were ratified and exchange of POW's took place and the war stopped. Withdrawing to pre-war positions was also agreed. All but any progress made in the core issue of the disputed territory of Kashmir The treaty has not been mentioned in any discussion on Kashmir and it seems it died with the sad parting of its stalwart author, Mr Lal Bahadur Shastri.

There have been other agreements like the 'Kashmir Accord' between Mrs Indira Ghandi and Shiekh Mohomad Abdulla in which legal changes were introduced to bring Kashmir closer in the fold of Indian constitution. Mr Abdulla was now a chief minister, demoted from his last position of a prime minister. There was no peace content. Lahore declaration signed by the, serving Prime Ministers of India and Pakistan, Mr Vajpai and Mr Nawaz Sherif, stipulated the willingness of a no-war pact and meeting at all levels between the two countries for resolution of all disputes, including Kashmir. A regular bus service was inaugurated between India and Pakistan, as a gesture towards peace. The romance did not last long and armed conflict in the mountains of Kashmir accelerated in pace and intensity leaving the subcontinent back in the realm of raging flames. One more blow was delivered to the subjectivity of people in Kashmir, because at no stage so far, did they feature in any of the agreements signed and their subsequent fate was decided for them as non-entity.

The prospects of accords succeeding have received a setback by the current revival of civil war in Jerusalem and Ghaza (November. 2000). There was a lot of hard work behind the peace process in Palestine, and yet exponents of peaceful co-existence have been defeated. I am tempted to take comfort from a free intellectual inquiry of making a comparison between Palestine and Kashmir. Parallels drawn indicate in essence that Kashmir differs in respect of hard division of religions antithetical to each other in Palestine but similarity in the disputed territories. In Kashmir there is a universal monolith image of some kind of freedom, a perception of individualism and subjectivity, some kind of identity that people are seeking rather than material or religious gains. If only a camp David type of accord became a reality, parties in dispute would comply and a new beginning made to arrive at a final treaty for peace.

India has offered a degree of relief to people by recent Assembly elections (2002) in which perceptably a dark cloud was lifted. People however are hoping that the process will continue for a successful resolution of their troubled destiny.

Pakistan has also concluded their parliamentry elections and a new government is in the making. It may be an era of new thinking will prevail and over-run all old half-cooked agreements.

Conjoint Rule

South Asian Community/Collective Security/Asian Military Alliance (AMA)/
Shared-Pooled Sovereignty

Asian Parliament

Assumptions: If what Plato said, it is true that the world was made from forms like Kashmir, live and innaminate objects, birds or trees brought together by ideas like virtue, then we can assume that the governments of South Asia would share power in Kashmir and influence the basis for collaborative regionalism and collective security. Organisation for Security and Co-operation in Europe (OSCE) has 50 members and works on the principle of collective security. Likewise, South Asian Community represented by a parliament may, it is hoped, enlist all regional states and become a credible force. Collective security ensures safeguards against incursions into each others' territory and would have strict code of practice and rules of behaviour agreed in a treaty. Balance of power politics as adopted by India and Pakistan is ill-suited to deal with conflicts that threaten regional peace and security. A regional collective security forum works best between democracies and we have to assume that Pakistan is potentially a democracy even though there are military take overs interceding periods of democratic governments. It must be emphasised that a state cannot claim credibility if a corrupt guided democratic process has underpinned it. In no uncertain terms it is Asian parliament and organisations like the OSCE which are geared up to help countries who face problems in keeping a hold on democratic institutions. Russia and the USA signed a charter in Istanbul on 19th November, 1999, for 'peaceful resolution of conflicts'. Russia even agreed to allow observers into Chechnya. It was agreed that OSCE will take the responsibility to look after conflicts in Eastern Europe. It is argued that a turbulent subcontinent like South Asia does have a need for OSCE type of an organisation. The question arises if it will be accepted and have a chance to work under the shadow of an imminent nuclear and missile warfare.

It may sound too idealistic that global governance will permeate through into South Asian Nations, now risen up to the standards required for maintenance of social justice, abolition of structural inequalities and an end to strife. Association of South East Asian Nations 'ASEAN' is not truly representative of South Asian subcontinent. Organisations like Asian Pacific Economic Corporation (APEC), South Asia Free Trade Area (SAFTA) and South Asian Association of Regional Co-operation (SAARC) also have minimal influence in crafting inter-state relations, resolution of conflicts and running of economies in South Asia. In November 1999 India, Russia and China met in Almaty under the banner of Conference for Intervention and Confidence building measures in Asia (CICA) and resolved to wipe out terrorism from its 3.5 billion people. The concept of regional solidarity was exemplified by Zimbabwe's President Robert Mugabe who managed to get South African president Thabo Mbeki and all other African leaders to support his position of illegal eviction of white farmers, otherwise untenable in international relations. Africa 2000 Forum have pledged a joint stock exchange and economic solidarity. A regional forum of culturally close concept of citizenship would imply rights and responsibilities to the union of every citizen. (Gultung).

Taking the subcontinent of South Asia as 'unit for analysis' the total population share ingredients of cultural similarities, language, demographic, economic and political problems specific to them. They became free nations about the same time and suffer limitations of decolonisation. Neo-colonial elements survived to support powerful fascist institutions and abuse progressivism. Politicians are subsumed in this process and guided democracies have preoccupation in pursuit of power by escalating conflicts. Kashmir is seen as a part of the family of Asians, therefore, it is argued, it takes more than its share of problems. In this paradigm, one is tempted to emulate European model. Chancellor Schruder of Germany recently made a revelation that a bi-cameral European parliament would create a new second chamber in which the heads of states would become members and invoke changes salient in their domestic policies. Likewise PM Vajpai could sit in a chamber in Srinagar and get economic or political perks for India.

Blueprint

The Asian parliament would base their offices in Kashmir on the same pattern as Brussels for Europe. This institution will have relevance to the concept of homogenesis seen in the populations and as a central agency exercising control over a melange of societies that do not claim to be a seamless, monochromatic garment. Kashmir dispute will be pacified and may become an issue for the Asian parliament to resolve. Help may be made available to players in the field of interactive conflict resolution and face to face complementarity. It may be agreed to sanitise all civilian territory and decommission weapons. Concerted work would start to bring all parties together to formulate a consensual solution to the Kashmir dispute. Kashmir will host such a parliament within its beautiful surroundings and offer a taste of their traditional hospitality. The parliament will be constituted on similar pattern as the European model. It is expected all contentious issues will be prioritised and the institution given the status to exercise its influence as a federalist entity. Members will see reason to co-operate and work in conformity as benevolent neighbours and solve all ethno-political skirmishes.

A visionary spectacle for the locals! Srinagar secretariat building would have flags of India and Pakistan fluttering side by side along with flags from Bangladesh, SriLanka, Nepal, Bhutan. The parliament will have the composition of members, (MAP'S) from all countries. A local administration for Kashmir would be formed by the parliament comprising technocrats and executives helped by the Indian and Pakistani experts. Local trade and commerce would be encouraged and links with all member-countries would open up with free flow of traffic and currency. A timeframe would be set up to allow all political parties to establish their mandates and future political relationships.

It is expected that the army presence will reduce and militant organisations will lay down arms. One model which may be a

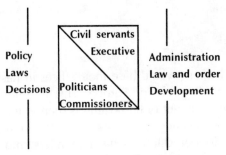

Role of politicians and executive

suitable blend between the paradigm under discussion and other forms of conjoint rule may take guidance from the European Union. The emphasis would be smooth inter-governmental relations and art of living within the Union. The politicians in the parliament would be expected to exercise control in four different forms. Political decision making, military deployment in maintaining a balance of defence and collective security, economic contractual relationship and cultural normative behaviour. Political milieu of amity will be conducive to reparation process to begin in Kashmir, and in other parts of South Asia with help from international agencies and NGO establishments.

Functional Strategy

South Asian community alliance not only reflects a proactive interaction between people but also nuances in political ideologies in the region. It may relieve a proportion of burden from the United Nations which is hobbled by conflicts with vested interests of superpowers and the fall out from cold war with little time for problems far afield. That is why the secretary-general said that the United Nations should look more frequently to regional structures and possible virtues of local multilateralism (Ghali Boutros). Based on the principle of multi-lateralism, the regional parliament will create space for governments to formulate policy towards each other, space for people to think with teleological ethics and for the world community to assimilate its benefits. India and Pakistan will not be losers, politically or economically. On the sensitive issue of security, optimism may prevail and the creation of an Asian military alliance (AMA) becomes a reality. In this model the NATO parallel springs to mind. This alliance equates to a treaty which may be the basis for a regional security umbrella in the subcontinent. Recent launch of an European army may cause a stir in Washington, but President Chirac and his followers believe in regional autonomy and not in unipolar or bipolar world.

It may be East Asia will also form a rapid reaction force possibly China at the vanguard position. In linking the security of states together, they implicitly avoid war against each other by seeking to mute security dilemma and by integration of a process of peaceful change. In line with the thinking of collective theorists we will indulge in our dream of Indo-Pak peace and pledge that force will be renounced and Kashmir dispute settled amicably. As a corollary, they may broaden their concept of national interest to take into account the interests of the regional community. A standing regional organisation will overcome the fear which dominates the political relations between India and Pakistan. The mere presence of nuclear weapons on both sides works against any efforts to engage in a debate based on mutual trust and respect for each other. Wisdom may prevail on South Asian neighbours entrusting their destinies to collective security notwithstanding the hard boiled Realists digging their heels on the scene in order to hijack reconciliation.

The parliament itself would be seen as an imperium of regional nation-states administering Kashmir for an interim period. In the timeframe people participation will be sought and gradually Switz style Cantons established from the grassroots to offer democracy in stages. It is hoped that people will be encouraged to interact with the political change. Nicole Ball (1996, p619) summarised the concept saying that peace agreements provide a framework for ending hostilities and a guide to initial stages of post conflict reform but they do not create conditions under which the deep cleavages that produced the conflict are automatically surmounted. In order to heal the social wounds work has to be done to shape interactions among citizens of all three parts. In my view people by and large will be receptive to early reconciliation between them. Spurred by the elements of homogenesis, I know they are ready for the change. In the construction of a model for collective security lessons have to be learnt from OSCE and operational methods emulated. The AMA collective security can set up a steering committee just like the contact group established in Bosnia and this committee will be given the task of solving not only problems between states but also inside each state.

Advantages

Whichever way you turn in South Asia a virulent conflict is staring in your eyes. The causal relations can be traced to multitude of factors. The inevitable aftermath of decolonisation, imperfect guided democracies, in the states, poverty, over population, utilitarianism, clientalism, exploitation, corruption, environmental and political migration, visceral caste systems, ethnic strife and many other factors have been activated in our immature nascent state polities, with the result that there are cries of freedom and rebellion everywhere. These are problems almost insurmountable by a state on its own especially if it is surrounded by enemies on its borders. In such circumstances it is logical to form a cohesive alliance with other countries in the region, rather than reach out to superpowers far away for help. Collective security would not implicitly be pre-occupied in maintaining a status quo but interact in disputes and like OSCE Helsinki Final Act, stimulate peace efforts. This will in practice mean inviolability of borders between the states and Human Rights, a common concern for all. Citizens will come out winners with Liberalist progressivism secured for all.

India can exercise hegemonic power in a more effective manner. This fact can be explained on the back of the Marxist theory which explains how winning the consent of people it subjugates makes it a better alternative to coercion. (Antonio Gramsci 1891-1937). India will maintain semi-control over all strategic points of entry and exit, provide safe passage to pilgrims and settle migrant Hindus back to their homes.

Military Alliance (AMA) would ensure collective security and its economic benefits. Politicians will get time to build bridges for peace and regain confidence of people from all parts of Kashmir. Collaborative growth industries and cross-border regionalisation of trade and commerce will stand in high regard in international markets. Sustainable development sectors will get a boost with Indian superiority in technology sector and the burgeoning supply side of economy in other parts of the region.

Pakistan on the other hand would be an important actor in the day to day running of the State. In the parliament they will have a right to privileges which will enable them to strike deals over water, forest products and transport in much the same way as if they had revived the agreement that existed in 1947 with Maharaja on postal services and exchange of commodities. There will be a free flow of citizens from both sides. Pakistan will be a part of the administration ruling Kashmir. The collective security will give Pakistan vital resources the country needs so urgently. It will also dispel the fears of the West of a nuclear input into the Arc of Islamic Menace by Pakistan, More so with significant gains by Muttahida Majlis-e-Amal (MMA) in general elections (oct. 2002) percieved to be anti-American. Economic benefits will accrue by, removal of sanctions and restraints on inward investment and bring prosperity in their society.

In the flurry of this activity people of Kashmir will become a focal point of attention and remain pivotal in the region. The tourist industry will thrive and Kashmir will no longer be a liability on India or Pakistan. It will provide a holiday destination for foreign tourists who will include places in India and Pakistan in their itinerary, benefiting the whole subcontinent. For the first time in many years normalcy in sustainable developmental projects and progressivism may get a chance. The potential for growth in industry, mining and urban agrarian development will be exploited. There are half a million educated and skilful Kashmiris the world over waiting to return home. That reverse migration would be a payoff in the supply side of economy.

Feasibility

Establishing an Asian Parliament will not give participating countries the automatic right to ownership of the place, yet at the same time by the mere presence of army and additional acts passed by the new parliament there would be safeguards to the suzerainty status for both India and Pakistan in their respective territories with additional benefit of having a control over the territory that was not under their direct rule. The knock on benefits from a central agency controlling economy in countries in the region will be significant.

Future

Asian parliament will have judicial powers to over-rule the decisions of the local judiciary of the states in matters of human rights, discrimination or corrupt practices inherited from their feudal systems. There will be breathing space for all political parties in Kashmir and a stronger relationship may develop with parties in India and Pakistan. Economic integration on a regional basis would contribute to erosion of militant nationalism and mitigate high strung attitudes of nation states. Time with peace is a great healer and influx of globalisation will make hard borders less important. A process of post-settlement peace building program would be set in motion at great speed. It may be that every facet of governing the place, inviting world governments for assistance and NGO's to work inside will gather pace. There is nothing analogous to peace in this strife-ridden world and we can give 'peace' a chance to work. Nationalism plays an important role in South Asian politics, notwithstanding hot pursuit of modernity and globalisation. As an indication to disprove this aphorism economic integration in Europe has been a main factor in the erosion of nationalism and redundancy of the concept of nation state. (Hassner). This kind of triumphalism could be replicated in Kashmir politics.. All countries in the region will work with each other rather than against each other and may give their people a better standard of life.

Shared Pooled Sovereignty by India and Pakistan: Place of Pilgrimage/Corporation

'The operating principles of Touheed

are Freedom, Equality and Solidarity' (Qur'an)

I have no doubt my critics will be hiding a derisory smirk at my figments of imagination. I will offer them comfort and admit that my whole set of paradigms package is based on probabilities and political dreams but I would also remind them that enlargement of the spectrum of alternatives must be indicative that we can deviate from the inflexible path of violence and recalcitrant stand-off. In much the same way as clash of civilisations has been described, a clash of egoistic utopias in my view can be blamed in part for conflict in Kashmir. India and Pakistan have a dream for Kashmir. The Concepts may not harmonise with the ideal visions of the people of Kashmir. Utopia for one party may turn out to be a nightmare for others.

It may therefore be useful to combine all parts of Kashmir into a single entity and made into a house of conjoint activity. A treaty drafted and ratified by India and Pakistan will ensure their respective political supremacy, but restricted to common use of Kashmir as a place for pilgrimage or a base for economic projects, research and development centres, a common tourist and recreational paradise or indeed a corporation managed by MD contingent from India and Pakistan. In this prototype, people of Kashmir would have a secondary place in governance but they will benefit from the activity generated by the two countries and enhancement of their lifestyle through progress. Their security will be assured because the two adversaries will be friends and their role will transform to benefactors.

Taking a lead from Montevideo convention, in order to club together one facet of their governance, for India and Pakistan, their own sovereignty will not be influenced or have any bearing on their own territory, populations, governance or capacity to enter into international relations. On the other hand the reality of the reliance on the historic exchange of polemics between India and Pakistan and recent wars, the most crucial element of the political association will be bringing the parties closer on matters of defence. Defence in real terms is power and control notwithstanding equally important other pillars of governance like Foreign Affairs, Communications, Economy, Home Affairs and Judiciary. In shared sovereignty of Kashmir, it is possible for India and Pakistan to share the four components of political power by taking responsibility for two each with built-in safeguard to avoid clash of interests for smooth running of the government. Social services and education could be entrusted to local governments elected on regional basis. I have been grinding away the thought of collaborative rule in Kashmir, well aware of the critique from Hobbenian club advancing the belief that only absolutism can guarantee order and social stability (Thomas Hobbs 1588-1679). Sovereignty does not tolerate higher or lower power and sharing it would be a contradiction in political terms. However, we have to charter all avenues for a chance to pool sovereignty and seek common good

Place of Pilgrimage

In order to conceptualise the paradigm, we have to rely on the theories of homogenises in human nature as the bedrock of political thought. It will be assumed that political association (governments) work towards the supreme good of people. Aristotle explains why happiness is the ultimate end of human action. Face to face in a shrine with God overlooking their objectives, will India and Pakistan still vow to kill each other? Eudaemonia leading up to progressive lifestyle and well-being for all, taken as a target in good politics would accommodate metaphysical compromises, no matter how difficult. Aristotle postulates that we as humans have particular functions as sculptors, fathers, doctors, husbands, soldiers etc; nevertheless we also have a function which goes beyond or transcends these roles. I think it is our devotion to God. I identified Kashmir with a spiritually charged haven, treated as a place for pilgrimage with very high ranking shrines representing all religions (Siraj).

Mr Clinton advanced a similar proposal for East Jerusalem in Camp David (19th July 2000). Israel and Palestine are engaged in a precarious debate about who controls it and both claim it as their capital. The place has religious and emotional significance. Mr Clinton made the suggestion that the place be venerated and governed under shared sovereignty. The idea being that Holy places like Lords in France, Mecca or The Vatican or Jerusalem should be only under His supreme rule and local administrators share duties as caretakers. Kashmir is also a sacred place for Muslims, Hindus and Buddhists. This paradign will provide free access to all its shrines in the event of a shared political control. A couple of years ago, ninety people were killed, most of them the Hindu pilgrims travelling to Amarnath Yatra in Kashmir. What is there to safeguard against future massacres of this kind? A contentious and muddled political structure makes a ground ripe for such atrocities. More force may not be the answer.

In the final analysis of the topic, the Vatican model has a track record of making an autonomous place of God for Gods' people and runs as a City without state intervention from Rome and stands as a real polity in its own right. The advantage to India and Pakistan to see Kashmir as a Holy place of pilgrimage, gives all their communities the best chance of carefree pilgrimage to Holy shrines combined with the holiday of a lifetime. There will be technical hurdles to cross in the event of an agreement by all parties. India and Pakistan have parts of Kashmir in their sovereign fold. They both have foundational doctrine of international law on their side guaranteeing their territorial and political integrity enshrined in UN charter Article 2(A). It may be they have to cede territory before it is shared.

Two Kashmirs Work as a Corporation

Citizens Rights to self preservation cannot be completely transferred to state, State itself needs citizens for its preservation (Spinoza 1632-677)

Corporation is a term normal in business and would imply an association of individuals, created under authority of law and will continue to exist irrespective of its members. India and Pakistan would be represented by directors, and governance will take the form of a neo-liberalist political association of mixed composition. In this political system with a corporation at the apex of the organisational theory and neo-liberal tradition in a functionalist society, the state will have very little role to play. I recall, one such functionalist unit came into being in Mysore state in India where local imperatives like socialisation, education etc., were undertaken in an autonomous manner by people working in Arab states. Kashmir will be one corporation superseding Bill Gates Microsoft Inc. The driving force will be the market and efficiency. The salience of production, agriculture, industry and exploitation of resources in pursuit of modernity and globalisation will overshadow the hegemony of power. This paradigm for Kashmir has the benefit of historical customs of the syndicalist movement of early 20th century in Europe.

A corporative state is a conglomeration of producer units, who in turn will form the substance of the state through an internal confederation. In other words groups of people in similar professions will form parties which in turn will be represented in the corporation. In Europe they were dominated by fascist parties, but Kashmir has the benefit of hindsight and the putative regime would be the board of directors accountable to neo-liberalist political tradition. In many respects autonomous Silicon Valley units are springing up in many countries. Social justice, self-government and co-operative economy was an Indian concept of Radical Humanism made known by Manabendra Roy (Roy). It could be given a chance to work for Kashmir. Corporation Unlimited with countervailing powers would have multiple shareholders from all over the subcontinent and indeed from far afield.

In Sophia Antepolis, Europe's largest complexes in France, more than 20,000 corporations are represented within this so called 'Intelligent City. 'People work and live inside this utopian and city are kept away from stress and pollution.

They perform well, excel in their professions and display high levels of happiness. Kashmir as a conglomerate corporation like Sophia would have to be incorporated into global economic justice structures within the United Nations. It would be imperative to ensure international corporate accountability and safeguards put in place from being swallowed up, along with all its mighty mountains by a corporate alligator!

A corporative state comes as close as you can get to John Locke's vision of governance based on laws of nature and makes it possible to separate power between legislature, executives and judiciary (Locke 1632-1704). Locke rejected Hobbenian state tradition in which people are subservient to the elite in governments or armies or oligarchs or even guided democracies. People in Kashmir are fed up with having to eulogise impressive political leaders and go out and kill themselves for their sake. Instead they want to get on with their lives and participate in the benefits of the global progressivism and a fulfilled life. It was the traditions set out in the past that people are subservient to absolute state structures. It was argued that absolute state was essential to prevent dichotomy of anarchy and order, even in a liberal tradition (Thomas Hobbes 1588-1679). In my analysis of the view, some states these days are themselves responsible for creating disorder in the society and Kashmir is an outstanding example.

Away from ruminating on the philosophical perspectives, in the real world, I accept, we need the details of crafting the infrastructure of a corporation style of governing body where India and Pakistan can partake with a degree of satisfaction. The project involves a radical transformation of the existing instruments of governance in both parts of Kashmir. It is expedient to distinguish between the Societal Corporatism as proposed in this paradigm and the fascist authoritarian type promulgated by Mussolini for Italian society. Two governments of Kashmir from both parts will integrate their organised interests by Liberalist tradition from bottom up structures as opposed to Mussolini's model in which organic unity of the total population would be a prelude to unitary state control. In our search for a solution to Kashmir dispute, we are keeping the interests of India and Pakistan within the fold of possibilities. In the event of state control of the two sides akin to Mussolini's model, it would further divide the possible symbiotic relationship of the two Kashmirs we aim to achieve.

Three Commissioners

Assumptions: This paradigm is a close variant of the Asian Parliament and deserves a mention in its own right because this arrangement is a contingency measure which is meant to be short-lived. The ongoing conflict in Kashmir is an interactive process with an escalator, self perpetuating dynamic exhorted by marionette regimes and hyper-active resident army. In India and Pakistan hostile stereotyped imagery is rampant in all ranks of executives and their followers. Hyper-real world media plays down the intensity of the violence in daily events and detracts the world concern. Citing just one example, the Reuters agency reported 20,000 killed in Kashmir uprising in 1992, and that figure has not altered even though Amnesty International have put the figure at more than 40,000. The report also ends by stating that the conflict is in 'the only Muslim state in Hindu majority India', making the dispute look like a war of religions.

We have to recognise that powerful vested interests will forestall progress. Peace in the region may be the end of feudalist dynasties and their portages. Enemy images can be a product of the need for identity and dynamics of group behaviour. Identity and cognitive biases do not always contribute to conflict by stereotyped images (Stein). Asian people eulogise and consciously believe in leaders and famous academics of the world. Kashmir could be trusted to be governed by the chosen commissioners.

The Blueprint of this model is to dismantle the present form of local government in both parts óf Kashmir. Three commissioners will govern from one office. India and Pakistan each appoint one commissioner and one is elected from within Jammu & Kashmir. Election for the local legislature or a parliament and the representative commissioner for Kashmir may be fraught with difficulties but consensual diplomacy will carry the day. Elections would be supervised with no visible guns. Appointments to higher positions will be guided by meritocracy, away from clan culture. The commissioners will govern for 15 years in five year terms. The three would take their turn to be the presiding chairman who for the term in office will take the responsibility of the chief executive in the government. In 15 years the military presence will be reduced significantly and all political parties encouraged to hold peaceful rallies. Administration would be structured to be delivered to lower levels of executives /directors appointed in equal numbers by three parties and experts in different departments. Management of macro-economy would be in the hands of commissioners or Quangos working on behalf of their respective governments. Micro-economy at individual level will be managed by local state heads of departments. Indian and Pakistani currencies would be in circulation.

In practice Kashmir will have self-rule with diluted authority in governance. The hope is that order can be established by Liberty and fraternal care. (Peter Kroptkin 1842-1921). A lot of goodwill is imperative for the success of this functionalist state. Tourism will need a boost by opening both routes of traffic, Local industry will have to be revived and politics tamed down. The hyper-real media will be reproved if it continues to spur on hostile imagery.

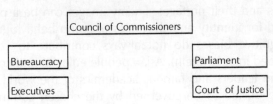

Government of Kashmir : Commissioners make decisions and legislate, parliament debates issues.

The dynamic of political change will bring confidence, axiomatic for a successful resolution of the dispute. The public will be taken into confidence, enabling important antecedents of governance like decommissioning of weapons by militants, and accelerated pace in developmental projects. Working practices will be written in a Treaty.

India may still keep its main military presence. The present rule by India is helped by its armed forces at great cost. The significant reduction will save money and save lives. The Indian flag will still fly over commissioners secretariat and India will have additional control over Pakistan administered Kashmir, with its civil servants having access to all parts of the state. In 15 years, people of Kashmir may even accept the presence of this model of government and vote for renewal to a further period of 15 years. In the duration of this time people will have been better educated in the pro-active politics and have insight into an ultimate solution which will determine their destiny. They could even lean towards more affiliation with India in the event of their benevolent behaviour and amicable relations.

Pakistan will partake in the administration of the total state and a free flow of its people into the Indian administered part will become a divination for which great emotions of joy will be displayed by separated families. Pakistan will also reduce army significantly and forestall a downward spiral of economy. Their presence in administration will hearten all friends of Pakistan. It is the civilian space created which will be crucial to people in the subcontinent and enable them to make judgements over their future political relationships.

Equalitarian justice delivered to people of Kashmir by any political change which helps to build the civil society and provide them security, opportunity, law and order, prosperity and a breathing time to build a better future for themselves, will be welcome. They will have respite from battering and humiliation inflicted on them by the very people who offer them unreserved patronage. Children having grown up in an ambience of terror and egregious suffering will surface to be nurtured into useful peace loving citizens. Fragmentation of power will help defend liberty and keep tyranny at bay. There would be subsidiarity of power, with multiple access points to establish institutionalised links with lower levels. That is the kind of democracy people like.

This modality of governance is built on consensual politics. The important phase in the government would be supreme decision making. The executives will deliver governance based on the qualified majority voting in the parliament. India and Pakistan both can sell this 'way out' of the present morass to their people and the world. India will be vindicated to a large extent and claim that they still have their army inside Kashmir and Pakistan can offer their people the first holiday of a life time in Kashmir and play an important role in the governance of the disputed region. It is possible both countries will get financial support from the international community and aid agencies to make the peace process durable. There may be shades of darkness in this process of relativisation, the hope is that a simultaneous ray of light from peace in the region will illuminate the patches. Other conflicts in the region are inter-related and will drop out as a by-product of peace in Kashmir.

Partial Autonomy:
Combined Kashmir/Divided Kashmir

Assumptions:

You will have realised by now that there is a common central theme running through the core of my thesis on alternatives and I will admit that some modalities do feature figuratively repetitious. Nevertheless, at the heart of the argument is the concept of exploring new avenues and new goals in the peace process. In pursuit of action theory, the beaten path is avoided in our situation. Partial autonomy is a known concept and may derive credence from the Belfast Treaty. In easing out hard rule to a community and sharing or pooling sovereignty, it may be that legislative devolution becomes a need and local laws, local legislature and fiscal independence becomes axiomatic to combat centri-fugal tensions. Let us take the paradigm further and analyse ways it becomes a reality. There are two distinct routes this paradigm can be used to deliver and made to work.

Combined Kashmir and Partial Autonomy.

As a new dispensation in the political lives of people from both parts of Kashmir, they would be given a chance to unite after 55 years. They would accept India and Pakistan to exercise joint suzerainty over the unitary region reconstituted as Jummu and Kashmir. In working out a blueprint for this paradigm all modalities of foreign policy including security, trade, diplomacy and development. Co-operation strategy would need to be crafted in conformity between all three parties. The executives of Kashmiri origin would run the daily business under the vigil of the policy makers from the federal headquarters of the two countries. This paradigm may be construed close to the three commissioners approach with the important difference that this arrangement may take a more lasting form. The state parliament would have the over all political control, encapsulating all sectors of Jammu & Kashmir with may be miniature sub-parliaments in places like Jammu, Ladakh, Gilgat-Baltistan or South Kashmir. Taking into cognisance the diverse nature of the minorities, the United Kashmir will be best served by a system of consociational system of government with territorial devolution, proportional representation and a grand coalition of power sharing democracy, incorporating Gigit-Baltistan, Ladakh and Poonch Districts. This model may address the concerns of pressure groups like Panun Kashmir or Gilgat-Baltistan Peoples Forum and others. There would thus be a three-tier hierarchy of a political umbrella devolving power and responsibility in a critical path of descending order. The functional strategy of partial autonomy will reside in the covenants in legislation featuring all concerns and requirements axiomatic to India and Pakistan. Executives from the ascendant countries will be received much like the British Residents were before 1947. Reflecting on the parody, if we spin history round in a full circle, we will be looking at the British receiving goats and cashmere shawls from Maharaja to mandate their supremacy from 1846. This time round fidelity will be owed to their brothers.

Divided Kashmir and Partial Autonomy.

A close variant of Independence, it is expected that India and Pakistan will loosen their grip on power and make their respective

Kashmirs autonomous. The two devolved parts of Kashmir will combine by treaty and the two local governments will work by merging social, economic and political disciplines. One strand of their foreign policy which will separate them is political parentage to India or Pakistan. Security will not be domestic to either state. It may be simple enough to visualise the present semi-autonomous country of Cyprus with the allegiance of North and South Cyprus to Ankara and Athens respectively. The two countries fought open battles for the Island, like India and Pakistan did for Kashmir. The Turkish and Greek parts of Cyprus have already collaborated in many projects and talks are under-way for closer ties. Supremacy of Greeks and Turks is not perceptible to people in Cyprus. Kashmir could emulate the pattern. Contextualising the paradigm further, one more example would be Korea. North and South having fought their battles and still under the influence of competing world powers, that has not stopped them from opening their borders and building new railway lines just so they will come closer.

In 1950 India came close to China and proposed a likening between North Korea and Pakistan, asking the United Nations to condemn Pakistan for invading Kashmir, if North Korea is blamed (Korbel). Political climate of the world has changed. It was inconceivable that an American president would visit Vietnam, having dropped seven million tonnes of bombs on its people. Vietnam shares its troubled history with Kashmir and merged its North and South into a single country, leaving behind a trail of footprints for Kashmir to follow. A step in right direction may be a change of the names of the two Kashmirs into West Kashmir and East Kashmir, instead of, Azad and Indian Kashmir, the strident reminders of the conflict. The line of control would be a trifling artefact with informal check posts permitting free flow of traffic and trade. Furthermore for both Kashmirs what matters as important is that the external influence on its peoples will be cryptic and imperceptible to their everyday lives and an end to the ubiquitous presence of military in the streets and gunmen in the bushes may become a reality !

India and Pakistan would not relinquish control of their regions and continue influence in the fields of macro-economy, communications, foreign affairs and defence. What makes this solution the most palatable from a lot of other options, is satisfying the ownership concept pervasive in Asian politics, at the same time as absolving the two Kashmirs from onerous responsibility of establishing diplomatic services and security arrangements. It may only be my dreaded fear, but I feel Kashmir will always need protection from invasions. Why not let the powerful nations on its borders be the custodians and save costs in the process!

I am tempted to call it a Federalist Quadrangular relationship to imply mutuality between the two Kashmirs, India and Pakistan. The union would be a part of broader Pluralism (James Madison 1751-1830). There will inevitably be tensions. It may be essential to establish multiple points of contact by institutions constructed from hybrid constituents. Pakistan will have access to the Indian Kashmir through trade, diplomacy and developmental collaboration. Both countries will share responsibility in selected disciplines. The passports will carry hyphenated identity as East or West Kashmir in the same way as say Hong Kong British did. Indian and Pakistani rupee will circulate as valid currency in due course. The two Kashmirs will work in the spirit of collectivism to foster solidarity and generate collective energy in economy and environment. In time both will draw more political power by acting in concert. On a spiritual level, they have a chance to exculpate each other from years of animosity, attrition and mutual assured destruction. This paradigmatic approach will appeal to the political language which enables them to qualify good rights, interests and ethical issues. Keeping in mind super ordinate goals, all parties have to work with positive inter-dependence, only then will their level of aspiration be realised. Two Kashmirs will harmonise, bringing peace into the realm of public domain.

Chapter

◄16►

Independence:
Modified Dixon Plan

Pursuit of Liberty may cause loss of Liberty, because it required protection by domination and control. (Pierre Joseph Proudhon 1809-65 : Anarchist).

Assumptions

There are blemishes to this paradigm which I must emphasise before I indulge in the vision of an independent Kashmir. There is an overall bias against Independent Kashmir, not only from the two big powers, parties in contention but also from other important institutions of the world politics. The guidelines set out in European Community foreign policy have relevance to events in Kashmir. It is stipulated that before a state is recognised as independent, the new state must demonstrate rule of law, true democracy, and more importantly safety and equal rights for national minorities. Can Independent Kashmir offer these guarantees to people of Ladakh and Jammu? The doctrine of Uti possidetis urges integrity of all sections of the society within the boundaries of the state. JKLF and other Independence seeking organisations would have to offer these pledges, if the solution will see the light of the day.

Is it realistic to assume that the long arm of NATO is not long enough to influence politics in Kashmir? Or does the truth reside, as already outlined in previous chapters, in the domain of international politics. As it happens, NATO members are also the world powers and determine the essence of the theory of international relations. They have rejected the idea of self determination and creation of new states, especially so with dominance of Muslim population. As if these constraints were not enough, there are factors in local politics which dispute independence for Kashmir. Kashmir, at this point in time, is construed as part of India and in part by Pakistan. Both use the United Nations foundational doctrine and the instrument of Charter, Article 2 (1) assuring their territorial integrity and political independence, notwithstanding UN recognition of Kashmir as a disputed polity. Mr J N Dixit, former Indian Foreign Secretary, believes Independent Kashmir would be land-locked. "They would have to depend either on India or Pakistan and that would create problems for them because if they decide to join one country, the other which will be rejected will create pressure" (Schofield). Trade embargo on Nepal reduced the country to vassalage. Kashmir would meet a similar fate.

Having played the devil's advocate and blighted the paradigm for Independence, it is also my duty to analyse the merits of a sovereign Kashmir. Paraphrasing the level of aspiration, people of Kashmir want a separate home. They have suffered abuse from despotism from as far back as history goes (Siraj). Independence is a credible option for them, supported by empirical, ethical and legal arguments. The antics of history lend support to the unitary nature of Kashmir. The powerful Buddhist, Hindu and Muslim rulers from Kashmir not only made Kashmir a credible kingdom but also took parts of India in their governing fold. Kashmir was declared independent by the British as a princely state and not included in partition of India. Economy of Kashmir, if managed properly, will sustain local needs. Kashmir is exporter of natural resources and manufactured merchandise which along with tourism kept a roof over the head of every citizen of Kashmir from times of recorded history. Handicraft exports from Kashmir were given Indian president's awards in recent years. Agricultural and forest sectors have a potential, difficult to match in the subcontinent. People have rejected the flaw in the paradigm of being land-locked. It is believed that limitation it imposes upon Kashmir will be overcome by trade-offs with India and Pakistan of land access to outside world with their use of rivers, vital to the economies of both countries. International conventions preclude states from blocking communication routes for land-locked places. Globalisation has trivialised the concept of rock hard state borders. Where is land access to India people ask? Given a chance and left alone by invaders, Kashmir will survive in a much better shape than other Himalayan states like Nepal, Tibet, Bhutan and Sikkim.

Self-determination : Prelude to Independence

In the event of no invasions from Pakistan and India in 1947, Kashmir would be an independent country today. The ruler had indubitably decided upon an independent status for the whole state (Lamb).

It may be my over zealous anticipation to draw an analogy with Thomas Jefferson's beliefs on Liberty and Rights of man. It was his creation of the populist movement in 1776 which underpinned the American revolution. Notwithstanding his doctrine discouraging violent struggle against the state or social and political upheaval, he did advocate a sustained struggle for independence from British colonial rule. The concept of self-determination was born and people in Kashmir for over half a century now have been ploughing through hard set ground of severe politics just so they can determine their own future. In the event they faced widespread victim derogation. The United Nations charter gives people sanction to claim statehood and determine freely their own political status. They can pursue economic, social and cultural development (ICCPR : International Covenant on Civil and Political Rights ; Article 1, 1966).

Deontological ethics would support self-determination in Kashmir, especially so because the people were promised a plebiscite to give them that right.

Notwithstanding the present utilitarian environment engendering commitment to 'what is in it for me' which precludes it, self-determination is a sacred sermon in modern politics. Kashmir has determinism emerging from interaction between conflicting parties, who are reliant on their needs to construct a multi-ethnic society. Both countries are aware of historical background when for instance on 25th July, 1947, Mountbatten proclaimed before the chamber of princes of India including Kashmir that " The states will have complete freedom; technically and legally they become independent" (Nicholas).

Assuming that people will vote in a plebiscite to be citizens of a free country, it would be easy to draw plans for execution of this solution. Independence of India act itself a product of liberation would lend itself as its precursor. Kashmir would replicate the procedures adopted by India and Pakistan in 1947. The new arrangement can be drafted very quickly. Both countries will withdraw their government machinery keeping a residual staff for smooth transition. The exit of the two it is hoped will not be doomed with violence or scorch earth policy. A local army will be derived from the existing armed forces in Pakistan, Kashmir and JK Militia, now serving under Indian army. In due course a democratic state will be created and all weapons in civilian hands decommissioned. The new government will have crucial issues both on domestic front and in their new place in the world, to implement. The challenges would be formidable to sort out the setting up of foreign office, laying infrastructure for utilities, communications, economy, defence and International relations.

In this paradigm India and Pakistan loose control of the whole state and both will have to recognise it as a separate country. A realisation may dawn that pursuit of superordinate goals like creation of a new country would have to involve both India and Pakistan in resources and effort. The flip side of the coin is that India-Pakistan confrontational rivalry will end and when one party perceives that their enemy has not won, it may be easy for them to accept conceding territory or as the phrase goes 'Land for peace' formula as applied in Palestine. In the functional strategy of the creation of this new country, teething problems will be faced. The saying goes that a fountain pen had to be borrowed from a Karachi hotel manager to sign the first government order in one of its rooms used to start running the country of Pakistan. Jammu & Kashmir has had so many governments come and go, it may be a task to dismantle some facilities deemed superfluous to requirement.

In any given situation India is in a position of superior strength and they can draw up a list of all facilities in communications, defence strategy, economy and rehabilitation of ethnic minorities on their agenda and use leverage for compliance. Indian position, claiming Kashmir as their integral part, would have been altered to conceding independence, and the policy would be commended as a paradigm shift.

Pakistan knows in its heart that independent Kashmir will predictably lean more towards that country in the long run because of the main arterial roads and a possible rail link, the flow of rivers and cultural exchanges with some kind of ethnic homogeneity. It is assumed that the support for this solution will be concordant with Kashmiri diaspora, wide spectrum of Indian and Pakistani intelligentsia and parties like JKLF and Kashmir Huriyat conference. Notwithstanding the challenges for the incumbent rulers of India and Pakistan to get consensus from people and spin doctors, there are factors which make this way out politically appealing. Apart from peace in the region, a new beginning would be made for progressivism, people from India and Pakistan would be enjoying holidays in Kashmir and governments would get all the economic benefits without having to take any responsibility for development and security concerns for Kashmir. A realisation will dawn in due course that conflict in Kashmir destroyed the psyche of organic folks in Kashmir and security forces of India and Pakistan. The daily fear of death and cognitive dissonance about clashing ideas tore them apart. Freedom could be on the other hand a prelude to anarchy. Vested interests, deeply entrenched in Kashmir politics may try foul play, because they will fear for their lives and future. Truth commission may be set up and amnesty programs implemented to obviate retribution and bitterness from fifty years of antithetical diatribe and conflict.

The anathema people of Kashmir have been dreading is a destructive civil war in the aftermath of independence, with glaringly example of Afghanistan as a point of reference in front of them. The task of reconstruction and reparation would have to be taken with robust determination. On the political front the independence enthusiasts claim that Kashmir would have to be cleansed of the flaws in foundations of democracy and avoid dark areas like juxtaposition of pluralism and clientelism, predominance of incompetent, ignorant and corrupt politicians and bureaucracts. Long history of forced poverty may push the politics to left of centre, neo-Marxist social democracy, espousing a culture of a welfare state.

Dixon Plan/Modified Dixon Plan

" I will find a way- or make one " (Peary)

Dixon Plan

The plan in its original form was the culmination of a series of modalities peddled by Sir Owen Dixon, Australian Jurist and UNCIP representative, in May 1950. In its final shape he crafted a divided state in which Jammu & Ladakh would remain with India. Pakistan would keep all parts in its control except Muzafarabad. Vale of Kashmir and Muzafarabad would decide their future through a plebiscite. It has been assumed that ethnic divide of the state may be conducive to an accepted solution. India and Pakistan would retain Hindu and Muslim majority regions respectively. The underlying argument used by Sir Dixon relied on the historical events of the partition of India on ethnic grounds and secondly the fact that Maharaja Gulab Singh had conquered and cobbled together the different regions in 1846 and created the state now called Jammu & Kashmir (Collins and Lapierre). This paradigm would in effect reverse Gulab's acquisitions and divide Kashmir into regions on ethnic grounds.

The outcome of this solution was that hopefully all parties will get what is legitimate to them. The armies of the two countries will withdraw from the valley and retain all other positions they hold at present. This model will revert Kashmir to indigenous lifestyle of each region. Culture and language are axiomatic to their identity which have characteristics peculiar to them. Considering teleological ethical elements, the society may live in peace isolated from each other, and reduce the stereotyped hostile imagery. The dis-engagement of armed forces from either country may release resources and the region may share the prosperity. In this solution the snag is that it was rejected at that time because both countries had high hopes of getting the total state as a part of their dominion. Is there a built in mechanism of conflict behaviour with degrees of ethnic heterogeneity which has reached a critical point at times of conflict and crossed the rubicon into violence?

For India leaving the Vale meant loosing the place for good. If there was a plebiscite, it would not be in their favour. On a sad note we will part company with Sir Dixon here. He left the subcontinent on 23rd August, 1950, tired and flustered. He wrote in his report to the United Nations, "There is I believe on the side of India a conception of what ought to be done about the real will of the people, which is not that tacitly assumed by me. Doubtless it is a conception which Pakistan does not share" (Korbel).

Modified Dixon Plan (MDP)

What we will now refer to as MDP, is a paradigm based on the foundational doctrine of Sir Dixon who worked very hard to provide the original framework. Modified Dixon plan in essence has the crucial ingredient of the 3rd option for the Vale-Muzafarabad region, and gives them the choice to govern as an autonomous entity with a loose frame constitution. Like the USA, laws can be modified by supreme court and by its affiliates. The other more important element in this new state (Kashmir Valley and Muzafarabad) would be to enter into special treaties and multilateral agreements on political, economic and defence matters with both India and Pakistan. This paradigm could be worked upon in reverse in a way that if the Vale Muzafarabad entity is made autonomous first and other regions demarcated and given an option to join India, Pakistan, or the Vale through a plebiscite.

India has extremist parties like Shiv Sena to accommodate and would like to retain bulk of its army in the region. They will continue to be the hegemonic power surrounding the valley and any time impose sanctions to achieve objectives. In MDP environment, tangible treaties will come into effect, offering benefits superseding the existing arrangements. Pakistan on the other hand will be politically vindicated, having got the Indian rule relinquished from the Muslim majority part of the state. There are prospects of long term relationship with the vale with mutual exchange of commodities and use of rivers and forest products. It is also realistic to assume that Pakistan will actively engage in cultural integration and Kashmiris now living in Pakistan encouraged to be resettled back in their native homes. Benefits would be shared in an equipoise manner. Theory of causal relations would validate claims of likely gains in fiscal terms and human resources for the whole region, if a change of political culture becomes a reality.

There are two important antecedent factors which will make this solution work. An intense activity in the markets of the region, open, interactive and unfettered. The second determinant of success will be free flow of people across borders like in European community. MDP offers a scope in the betterment of multilateral relations which underpins feasibility of a final solution of the conflict. The fact remains that a lot of water has flown under the bridge since Dixon plan was rejected and having altered its structure makes MDP a credible option. In Kashmir there is a positive bias against ethno-centricism, therefore cultural and trade relations may continue as before. The new states may form a self-governing association of members of civil society and even with divided territories use collectivism to self governing association of free individuals (Michael Bakunin 1814-76). On the moral front the interaction will foster social solidarity and economic prosperity with collective effort.

Chapter

◀17▶

Comparative Peace Process:
Trusteeship

Kashmir weds: There are ornaments in the politics of Nations of the world, which may be used to decorate the bride of Kashmir.

The case study of the countries given, depicts how their political system works despite having a different constitutional relationship with parent country. Some elements from these models could be used in Kashmir, in entirety or modified to fit into new circumstances.

Kashmir may be a pretty looking prodigy but she has to overcome the cognitive dissonance of choosing contenders in wedlock. Is it India, Pakistan, or both or none? If she weds one, the process of incompatible activities will accelerate. It may be that dogged pursuit of Hedonism will in the end destroy all three ! If wisdom prevails, lessons may be learnt from the experience of events in the world history of conflictual situations and political structural similarities to Kashmir. Having identified the usable components of politics, we can craft a final goal and work backwards to detail sub-goals as in a critical path mode. We can then allocate time and resources to make the paradigm work.

United Nations Role in Namibia

A comparison drawn between the conflicts in Namibia and Kashmir has been seen to show similarities. The attempts at reconciliation in Namibia and Kashmir have mainly been from

The United Nations agencies. In Namibia the United Nations used diplomacy and hard negotiation to bring the protagonists together. They put pressure on South Africa to accept the peace proposal. In the case of Kashmir the United Nations did manage to bring the parties together and deployed its commissions (UNCIP) into the subcontinent three times from 1948 to 1965. They failed to get a consensus on the conduct of the peace process, in particular the mechanics of holding the plebiscite. It was agreed that people must be asked to vote but like the South Africans in Namibia or Indonesians in Eastern Timor, India insisted that its army will stay in Kashmir to supervise the plebiscite. India has since held elections in Kashmir to a constituent assembly but like the South Africans held election in Namibia, this action was not recognised or validated by the United Nations in both instances.

It is assumed that South Africa agreed to withdraw from Namibia because it did not perceive Namibia to be a threat to its security. South Africa at the same time adopted a shift in its policy of international politics and favoured peace accords. The apartheid regime was under increasing pressure to relinquish their harsh policies. Namibia seemed less important. In Kashmir security threat continues to influence political relations and its people become the ingenuous prey of hostilities.

Could the components of the peace process in Namibia be replicated in Kashmir?

We will draw a comparison between the genesis and structure of the two conflicts :

Namibia was occupied by Germany and South Africa as a territory to settle Germans and then South African whites and for its diamond mines. Kashmir has been under control of India and Pakistan for 55 years and possibly for its resources and its scenic mountains.

Cold War had an impact on both conflicts. In Namibia the USSR and its allies and the West were involved through the Angolan war. In Kashmir all efforts by the United Nations to bring about a plebiscite were docked by the USSR. They exercised veto power to invalidate resolutions sponsored by the Western powers in order to antagonise them (Lamb 1997).

Wars ended up in a stalemate. SWAPO joined communist forces in Angola against UNITA and South African army. India and Pakistan fought two wars in Kashmir and both ended in deadlock.

SWAPO was recognised as a legitimate political party of Namibia by the United Nations, but Huriyat, the political coalition of 32 parties in Kashmir, is not recognised in the same way.

Occupation of Namibia by Germans and South Africa was recognised as an 'occupation' per se. Kashmir is recognised as a disputed territory in international relations / institutions but non-Kashmiri armies stationed inside are not decreed as occupation forces by International Court of Justice and the United Nations in the same manner as Namibia.

South Africa used Namibia as a base to fight a war against Angola. In Kashmir India and Pakistan fight each other on Kashmiri soil and disregard local casualties and ruin.

Both Namibia and Kashmir demanded self determination using the instrument of a plebiscite under the UN auspices. Namibia got its chance and Kashmir is still waiting.

South Africa and the UN did accept in principle Namibia as a nation state. Kashmir has not been recognised by India, Pakistan or international community as a separate entity.

Players in the complex Namibian war, UNITA, Cuba, Angola were all tired of the war and South Africa followed the suit, more so when its business community put pressure on their government to agree with peace proposals. All these factors were seen to be absent in South Asian politics. India and Pakistan are building their military might round the Kashmir dispute. All agreements signed by the parties to continue to solve the conflict in Kashmir have been reneged upon.

In order to evaluate chances of success, the peace process agencies in Namibia have been vanquished and in the first instance brought a negative peace to the region. There have been shortcomings in the rehabilitation of the freedom fighters and poor unemployed rural population. There is evidence of corruption in the government agencies and executives. The country remains poor but the elite have luxurious comforts including swimming pools in their homes. It seems the United Nations development agencies made an early exit from the country, like they did in East Timor and the consequences of the settlement were not dealt with. This would be a lesson for Kashmir to learn. If ever a chance for them came to have a plebiscite and they were liberated, the United Nations peace making agencies will have to continue with the task in the post-settlement period for a long time.

Namibia is a success story for the United Nations. What could be done to replicate the components of this peace process in Kashmir? The result of inquiry into the question may reveal that the United Nations had constraints upon it, when dealing with India and Pakistan. Namibia case had conditions which favoured its peace process. The contact group linked Cuban withdrawal from Angola with agreement from South Africa to an election. This treaty was signed in New York. These strands of political process involving cold war players were absent in Kashmir. May be if there was a re-run of events of 1948 or 1965 wars, Russia would not obstruct Security Council resolutions, especially now because of its involvement in Chechnya and its changing attitudes towards international relations. The United Nations may find other factors like regional alliances, fragments of globalisation and changes in the politics of a new world order more conducive to a new initiative on the lines of the Namibian model.

Namibia has severed links with South Africa and Germany albeit a large white population still remains as Diaspora and have accepted their present political position. In Kashmir people are so close to the populations in the subcontinent that such a divorce of communities is very unlikely at any time in future, whatever their position in the region.

Channel Islands (C.I)

Multilaterism and juxtaposition of kinship and devolution works for Channel Islands, why not for Kashmir?

The people of this group of five Islands, South of England, consider themselves as part of Great Britain, yet they have complete autonomy, their own constitution, electoral system, national health service, customs and excise and currency. They are not even a part of the European Union. It is possible to divorce the satellite country from as many rules and constraints of parent countries that apart from not having to obtain a visa to enter the country, it is a separate country in its own right. In C.I. a British citizen has no right to buy property or stay in the country without being employed. The C.I. ruling council admit into the country about five new persons every year to adopt citizenship provided they bring substantial cash and invest it. Kashmir could offer to settle ten millionours from anywhere every year. The Islands are nearer to France than Britain and French is freely spoken alongside English. The only concern people have is prosperity of their citizens, a utilitarian polity and cost benefit of economists dominates the governing doctrines. Kashmir polity will divorce from all political constraints, and invite the people of the world to share prosperity with India and Pakistan.

Functional strategy of these values for Kashmir will be a paradigm of self-rule in the shape of a local government elected in both parts of Kashmir and political power shared under the aegis of India and Pakistan. It will be a crucial landmark for the people to be given a right to franchise and to be able to vote without any constraints or strings attached to their expression of choices. It is important for people of Kashmir to feel in their hearts that first time in many years they will be treated with respect and as equal free citizens. India and Pakistan will have political influence in the running of administration notwithstanding a high degree of self-determination and rights offered to the people of the state. They will have a regulatory mechanism in unison with regional politics. That model may be beneficial to development and offer solutions to security concerns.

Northern Ireland

"We have no need for violence'" (people of Kashmir and Northern Ireland).

Joint sovereignty as a political tool was conceptualised in the Belfast agreement and culminated into a path for peace and to a degree rescind the notion of statehood. This analysis has a mirror effect on Kashmir. It is therefore a rational exercise to draw a comparison of the Kashmir conflict with Northern Ireland on the optimistic note that a solution is possible even in intractable conflicts. Kashmir does not match on equal terms with NI because the ethnic strands to the dispute are dominant in NI only less so in Kashmir.

The three parties in NI are the people of NI, Dublin and London, comparable to people of Kashmir, New Delhi and Islamabad. The assembly in NI was suspended for a time pending decommissioning of weapons by IRA and Unionist paramilitary groups. This paradigm will work as a stepping stone for peace in Kashmir and its aftermath a template for future.

Drawing on the NI experience the blueprint of a solution for Kashmir can be initiated by bringing the Indian and Pakistani negotiators together in order to put forward their mandatory needs and work out the mechanics of sharing control over Kashmir. Modalities would be discussed at an academic level, then progress to sub-state levels which in turn would prepare ground for the high level meeting and a final treaty drafted and signed. A local government for the combined state will be elected with both parts of Kashmir represented. Elections would take place under a joint control of India and Pakistan. The executive accountable to governments which delegate power to them will quickly be put together. The legislature may be introduced as a second echelon in the process. Judiciary may function in its present form, only more transparent and accountable ensuring maximum liberty with equal opportunity for all. All these functional elements will only come into practice once a treaty

Northern Ireland	Kashmir
Three party conflict	Three party conflict
Friday Agreement:: Power Sharing	Proposed agreement.: Power Sharing
North-South Ministerial Council	Indo-Pakistan Ministerial Council
to oversee political adminstration.	to oversee political adminstration.
New Anglo-Irish Treaty	New Indo-Pakistan Treaty
Amend Irish / British constitution	Amend similar eg. Article I (Indian)
Stay British by consent	Stay Indian/ Pakistan by consent
NI elected assembly inclusive of	United Kashmir elected assembly
all control, Police, Justice, Rights	control, Police, Justice, Rights, Adm.

has been signed by all parties and ratified by the incumbent governments. There will have to be a transfer of power, and assets from all sides. Details will need to be worked out.

The important common features are, devolution, joint control and demilitarisation.

India and Pakistan will have control over all matters important to them. Defence, communications and foreign affairs may be shared in some manner workable in practice. An amicable settlement will result where all disputants will partake and benefit from. All it needs is an understanding between the protagonists in the dispute that this can be a legal way out without infringement of their state constitutions They will exercise their audit of checks and balances and may be conclude that this method of resolution is best suited to them, in comparison to de facto impasse and violence. Fading of nationality would be evidenced in both the Irish and English viewed through the concept of joint sovereignty (Oscar Wild).

Future for this module will have similar prognosis as 'Shared Sovereignty' in Kashmir and advantages will be similar. It may be the local administration will have the help they need from both India and Pakistan needed to control civil disorder and armed renegades running loose and still engaged in disruptive activities. The subcontinent will be on road to quick prosperity and adopt the progressivist framework in their governing practices. Northern Ireland administration is facing problems, but both the republicans and Unionists have stopped use of guns and at last, the sworn enemies are seen sitting close and sharing governance of the devolved state. More important for its lead in Kashmir is active participation of Irish republic, in what would be a precedent for Pakistan's role in Indian Kashmir. In 1985 a pact signed between British and Irish governments gave the republic a consultative role in the running of NI. Following the trail of co-operation and peace effort the two governments issued the Downing Street Declaration which laid the framework for what we are witnessing today.

The lesson to learn for parties in the Kashmir dispute, is the unrequited efforts used in NI, over-riding the emotions stirred with violence against civilians. Violence it is understood was the result and not the cause of the conflict. NI made a gradual progress and kept options admissible, and its door open for personalities of the world to help in the mediation process. That paved the way and made the difficult journey in the peace process passable.

Costa Rica

" We have no need for an army,

We live on Amity, Free air and Faith" (M.S. for people in Kashmir).

Costa Rica is a happy oddity in Central America which prides itself in a stable democratic government and that has disbanded its army to preserve the peace. In drawing on the Costa Rican model to apply in Kashmir, absence of army from its soil and its geo-political landscape make striking parallel between the two. For Kashmir it would be like an utopian dream to even approach a semblance with Cost Rica, a small country furthest away and yet so close in similitude of geopolitical structure. If CR was the aspiration of the people of Kashmir they would have to be a buffer state between hyped up, high strung countries like China, India and Pakistan, in the same way as CR stands between Nicaragua and Panama, having signed a peace treaty with them along with El Salvador, Guatemala and Honduras in the region. There are limitations of a demilitarised state. Kashmir would not be immune from spill over of conflicts from across the borders or in case of CR drug traffickers. Albeit exponents of peace argue that advantages of rapid and sustained development would outweigh the limitations. CR is a bridge between the Pacific Ocean and the Caribbean Sea, two big waters of the world. Kashmir sits in the middle of Himalayas and Pamirs, the mightiest mountains of the world. Could they be a nexus for peace?

CR has a simple and effective political system. The president is elected for one four-year term only, the legislative assembly is elected and judiciary is appointed by the assembly. The striking features which may benefit Kashmir are that the assembly has co-equal powers and can over-rule a veto from the president. Assembly members elected for four years cannot be elected again and judiciary has a limited term of eight years. Such a system eliminates corruption, abuse of power, oligarchy and enhances accountability. Limitation for Kashmir may be that CR has 93 percent literacy levels which will be hard to match for Kashmir.

The annual income per head in CR is $ 4413, approaching a near 0.75 HDI (Human Development Index) for its 3.13 million population as against perhaps a dollar a day in Kashmir with zero HDI for its 12 million people. The dividends for CR are not just resources. It has to be peace and stable governments. If CR sells coffee, bananas and tourism, Kashmir also has lush green pastures, agriculture and handicrafts and like CR hydro-electric power which it can export. A third of CR is forested and export its products. Kashmir also has a forest terrain which if managed judiciously can be income generating. Tourism in Kashmir can be very profitable.

Some Other Regions

Cyprus has been mentioned in the partial autonomy paradigm and the point made about its significance for Kashmir rests mainly in its history, partition and rule by two feuding masters situated outside the confines of the country. Like Kashmir this Mediterranean Island has been host to gods, crusaders, saints, its heroes and many millions of holiday makers. The North and South Cyprus have been compared to Azad (West) and Indian (East) Kashmir. Cyprus is controlled by Turkey and Greece in the same way as Kashmir is ruled by Pakistan and India. Like Kashmir, the division in Cyprus was the end result of an open war. As for the future, the two parts of Cyprus are making progress at peace making independent of their two masters. There is a pro-active dialogue about political union between the two parts and joining the Europian Union is on the cards.

Vietnam faced 2.8 million American soldiers, 56,000 of whom died without achieving any objectives. It was the French who colonised it, followed by Japanese in 1940 who were defeated and under leadership of Ho Chi Minh prevented French re-entry. North and South Vietnam like Kashmir were divided by external forces. In the final outcome the country united in 1976.

Western Sahara and its phosphate deposits, invited occupation by Germans and Spanish and ended up divided between Morocco and Mauritania. Sahrawis declared independence, recognised by 70 states. UN Secretary General Kofi Annan takes interest far more in this region than he has given to Kashmir.

East Timore

This is the tiniest and the newest country of the world. It was given the official status of a country in April 2002. It was not long after the Portuguese left this Island, that Indonesia saw a vulnerable territory on their door step. They occupied it. In 1947, Kashmir was also unprotected and became a soft target. The United Nations has achieved success in having a plebiscite in East Timor, only because financial sanctions were imposed on Indonesia and Australia was prepared to deploy its forces to monitor the exit of Indonesian troops. For the United Nations this is a success story. The United Nations had the backing of the rich countries who pay their wages and the coloniser in this case was not a member of the elite political club. The plebiscite result was independence and the United Nations saw through the transitional period. Kashmir dispute will be resolved if the United Nations replicates the procedures adopted in East Timorh.

Trusteeship/Mandated Territory/Protectorate

Assumptions in this paradigm will mainly rest on a 'floating polity' for Kashmir, having untied its moorings and ready for navigational directions in order to straggle for journey ahead. It may be that its attachments which have incarcerated its progress in political oceans are too inflexible. There is a sound legacy which will underpin the concept of this model. After World War 1 territory released with the defeat of the Germans and the Ottoman empire was 'mandated' by the League of Nations who took on the role of trustees of these states. The victors in the war did not adopt the territories won, instead took on the mandate of the League to rule the states pending eventual self rule. France took the mandate for Syria, British for Palestine, TransJordan and Iraq. In Africa, Britain looked after Tanganyika and shared responsibility of Cameroon and Togoland with France. Namibia was placed in the hands of South Africa who tried to defy obligation to the United Nations and colonise the country. The United Nations played a pro-active role in getting independence for Namibia.

Kashmir would be a mandated territory in the trusteeship of United Nations and mandated to India and Pakistan, ideally suited to a shared mandate, as in the case of Cameroon and

Togoland. The area would be demilitarised and civil society streamlined into progress and prosperity. The United Nations would have to oversee the administration on both sides and borders opened to a free flow of people. An agreement with both India and Pakistan would be essential to detail the role of each country in the mandate. This would be mutually decided by all parties. The administration would be shared by India and Pakistan either in accordance with the territories controlled by them or a rule by joint representatives. The United Nations may play a part to oversee civil administration, development of the state and de-militerisation.

The paradigm will lend itself to implementation in conformity and within the rules of functional strategy in operation. The United Nations maintains its constituent organ of Trusteeship Council. This department has not been activated through lack of a call for its use. It is possible the Council would take up Kashmir issue on its business schedules and work on principles laid down for it by its erstwhile organisation, the League of Nations. Drawing from Namibian experience, the Council would have to put safeguards in place to avoid entrenched occupation all over again. The mandated system gave birth to the idea that these territories were a trust rather than a property to be exploited and treated as if the people had no rights of their own. (Easton 1964).

Considering the intensity of the conflict in Kashmir and the degree of destruction to life and property, this arrangement will bring invaluable advantages to all parties. Trusteeship in the post World War era set an important precedent to decolonise states. In Kashmir itself there would be a free movement across the borders, co-operation between the two countries to demilitarise the region including disarming all militants. People of Kashmir will embrace a normalised civil society in which political violence has been removed and rule of law restored.

Protectorate

As a protectorate, political status for Kashmir would in reality be a dependency of India or Pakistan to the extent of the territories under their control. Kashmir split in this way would be treated as a colonial vassal state. Eastern European states were protectorates of the Soviet Union and the semi-rule was peremptory with. Soviet military stationed in huge numbers Kashmir will render itself to the protective fold of its stronger parent state and will be partly governed by it, much like the British ruled Kashmir during Dogra regimes. This paradigm corresponds to the period during which Oliver and Richard Cromwell were in power in British history. This prototype of colonising paradigm may not be an accepted way out for people of Kashmir because it may not be an improvement on what they already have and then it may be a painful re-run of history with strident memories of totalitarianism days.

Rebuilding Kashmir:
Peace Keeping

" **When you look into the abyss,**
The abyss is looking into you" (Friedrich Nietzsche 1844-90)

Movement in politics for Kashmir has become important. If we want to avoid further atrophy and burn out, we need to leap over the abyss and make good not only damage to infrastructure and environment of the country, but also dismantling its developmental foundations which is its people. As people get killed or flee from violence and become migrants, they forsake their normal livelihood. Kashmir's socio-economic progress for a better living becomes extraneous and comes to a halt. Liberty has become a benchmark to rebuilding Kashmir, free from political strife and on its road to recovery. In order not to spoil the optimism, we ardently hope that all refugees and political fugitives of Kashmir, Hindus and Muslims, languishing all over the world would return home and provide the supply side of development process. Progress will be imminent. Kashmiri diaspora given security and opportunity will return home because they have left a paradise on earth behind with singularities in culture very close to their hearts. The fear is that second generation youth—the young talented people —and diaspora, some of whom have never even seen their ancestral home, may have dissonance in their allegiance, a conflict they harbour:

'I carry two worlds in me - But neither is a whole'.

It may not be feasible to expect transitional governments to furnish public goods, protect property rights, legal framework for investment and other requirements for economic growth. One most important problem in Kashmir would be the political structure of the government. It is unlikely that the conflict will ever end with one clear winner. The problems would arise about consensus on the direction, rebuilding measures would take. Drawing on experience from other post conflict situations even when reforms are mandated by peace accord, their implementation is uncertain since it is unclear who will be in control and what powers still reside with them. Afghanistan is one example which comes up at every stage of analysis. Civil society, institutions and epistemic communities of Kashmir have fragmented over half a century, at the same time as being devastated by violence. They will require active help from the donor agencies to spawn into a credible force as a support for progress.

Economic and social characteristics in Kashmir are atypical of other post-conflict situations. On macro level the forces of India and Pakistan operating in their parts of Kashmir had to keep those roads and communications in good repairs which are important for their own use. The same could not be said about healthcare, education, agriculture or industry. Similarly on the micro level, damage in real terms is almost complete dependence for food items on imports from India and Pakistan. Kashmir, a land of plenty at one time, has complete reliance on imported food and commodities because local production has ceased. In Kashmir a multilateral co-ordinated program will need to be framed from all donors of international aid agencies including United Nations Development Program (UNDP) United States Agency for International Development, IMF and World Bank and NGOs of world repute to implement regeneration programs.

Prioritising rehabilitation of victims of violence and rebuilding devastated infrastructure will be a task. Particular attention will be required in taking arms out of circulation. Institutional reforms, establishment of police and judicial system will need to be set up. It will be essential to make certain interests of all groups including non-combatants are represented, apart from social and economic development programs. In order for the societies of Kashmir to make a fresh start for a clean living, a full stock of the political good guys and bad guys will need to be taken through Truth Commissions and tribunals set up to deliver justice. Questions would need to be addressed about justice, human rights, needs of people including minorities, legitimacy of the government and mutual relationships of all parties, in order to complete the rubric of political theory (Plant).

Peace Building in Kashmir after a negotiated settlement..

Transition	Consolidation
Establishing a government with legitimacy which is consolidation and amicable coalition to rule effectively. The government needs to implement reforms, build political institutions and establish security and start economic and social revitalisation	Maintaining the reform process. Continuing economic and social recovery programs, using judiciously aid from all donors.

One of the major challenges for peace building process will be reconciliation of a melange of political groups from both parts of Kashmir. It may be argued, why in the face of a violent revolution with 'Political Freedom' as a common objective have so many divergent views emerged? In drawing experience from conflicts in other countries, it has been observed that some of the antagonist groups were created by states as strategy to weaken the revolt and ideology which exhorts militancy and ebullience with similar goals. Consequently as events unfold, such groups were actively promoted in Kashmir to frustrate the movement. Nevertheless they will continue to exist even though their role is no longer needed, a fact the managers will have to take on board when rebuilding institutions of power.

In the Peace Settlement acted out in some other conflicts, they did not address the consequences of war, rehabilitation of political detainees and rural population. Lessons learnt have to be foremost in our minds. Wherever you go any place like Kupwara, Sopore, Doda or Baramula, signs of devastation are in evidence. Rows of shopping arcades have turned into a heap of brick and mortar. At the same time, there have been widespread, unregulated, monstrous buildings mushrooming everywhere, stimulated by political fake money, and inane attitude of local authority. Lack of direction or the will to impose regulations in the face of militancy is an excuse used.

In reversing the damage done to environment, infrastructure, indigenous economy and the fabric of the society, a comprehensive program would entail laying structures of organisational institution and a check list of priorities to work from. Kashmir is poor and with increased needs it is poorer still. The initial period of restoration will require help from external agencies like UNDP, IMF, IFAD, UNICEF and the world Bank. People have lost touch with the culture of work and production. They will need to participate in a national crusade for a green revolution. Farms and more farms, planting trees and more trees, growth in all areas of agriculture, horticulture, industry in both handicraft and mechanised sectors. Water resources and power generating sectors are under-exploited and require skilled management. Public utilities are sketchy and have taken a second place to state's pre-occupations in security matters. Measures need to be taken to combat spread of disease, social deprivation, illiteracy and un-employment. In an effort to sum up broad based agenda of peace building in a supposedly post settlement phase of Kashmir, it may be worth an endeavour to reframe the conflict. The feuding parties can no longer remain pre-occupied in focussing on issues in a direct, cognitive manner. It may be that various levels of contact are exploited to redress the painful past.

A position of peace and reconciliation and means of dealing with the present for a shared prosperous future is the ultimate goal.

Conclusion & Epilogue

Whoever does not waste his allotted time on Earth is in no danger:
His own light will show the way : (Pythagoras 570-500 BC).

It may be an unattainable utopia to conceptualise Emanuel Kant's perpetual peace in the region with colossal heterogeneity in political thought servile to hardened attitudes and to some extent esoteric beliefs. What did Kant mean by moral imperative? How would it have any relevance to the dispute in Kashmir? Taking lessons from his teachings, prescient to a final outcome of the dispute, Kant would make politicians responsible for the escalating conflict and not acting rationally above instinct and self interest. That would be a virtuous act, only expected from virtuous people. This work has tried to underpin assumptions that parties in conflict make a response on factual informed understanding of the sources of conflict. In order to achieve results in a difficult situation like Kashmir the inquiry has dwelt on exploring palatable alternatives to hardened policies of incumbents.

India and Pakistan will have to take three steps back to make room for peace, Prosperity and Progress towards collaborative regionalism. India accuses Pakistan of occupying part of Kashmir and argues that Pakistan withdrawal from Kashmir must precede any talks on settlement of the dispute. Pakistan on the other hand maintains the position that both parts of Kashmir must be demilitarised simultaneously and a plebiscite held to allow people to decide their future under the aegis of United Nations.

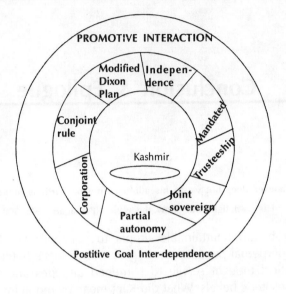

PROMOTIVE INTERACTION

Modified Dixon Plan
Independence
Conjoint rule
Mandated
Trusteeship
Corporation
Kashmir
Joint sovereign
Partial autonomy
Postitive Goal Inter-dependence

Peace Wheel for Kashmir (M S)

Notes :-

1 Promotive Interaction (PI) = Members engaged in peace process, encourage and facilitate each other's efforts to complete the task. The task may be as difficult as ' Who gets what from Kashmir '?

2 Positive Goal Interdependence (PGI) = All parties link together to make a joint effort. The policy adopted dictates that the perception members have is that they can achieve their goals if and only if the others in the dispute also attain tangible benefits. In Kashmir, PGI would indubitably rest on solutions where all get a share.

The last meeting in Lahore now called Lahore declaration and the follow up tract II diplomacy initiated by Neorana group and Niaz A Naik, the former Pakistan Foreign Secretary, would be a quantum leap forward towards peace. In negotiations held so far, the delegates meet with civility, enjoy hospitality and humour only to end up even more aloof and talking past each other. A unit analysis of these negotiations witnessed the unfocussed nature and confusion in definition of definite goals before the teams.

The aim must be to work towards a composite dialogue between foreign secretaries and set a format and agenda for a summit to sign a peace deal. One such meeting took place in SAARC summit in Colombo. There were no set of proposals to explore common ground to work on. In the event they agreed not to agree on fundamental issues and decamped with an assumed smile for the waiting press outside. The brief for the negotiators was based on policy set in concrete many years ago. More violence breaks out with vicarious consequences for people in Kashmir, who are not even a part of the aborted negotiations or if we go back to the genesis of the conflict, played any part in its causal relations. The frustrated agencies load down their fury on them and inflict harsh treatment indiscriminately. The half hearted attempts by echelons of power at holding talks with partisan militant groups in isolation are unlikely to make any progress in making peace. Both sides have an agenda which is in variance with actual peace making. They want to be seen to be doing something in order to satisfy the diplomatic and domestic concerns. It is my case therefore that actors in the process need to make policy changes, away from the beaten path already adopted.

Our contribution in this discourse has rested mainly in offering a road map towards that end. I am convinced that some where, some one, in some elite offices are making some mistakes. I also agree with the Indian position that solutions have to be home grown and forthright. Bill Clinton's visit to South Asia, apart from bestirring more senseless massacres of Kashmiri civilians, did not provide new initiatives for peace. In my view, if we had initiated a process of exploring alternatives before Clinton arrived, he might have contributed in narrowing differences. We were expecting Clinton to intercede and wave a magic wand to solve the conflict. One has to understand that with the finest intelligence about the conflict and imbued with primacy of human rights,

Clinton could only offer Liberalist solutions. It was apparent he did not even try. To him, one American citizen's life lost in political violence, can alter policies in White House or the Congress. In Kashmir human bodies float in rivers and are seen dumped outside the doors of their relatives on a regular basis. How many People from all sides killed in action and army get and who has ever shown an impassioned concern for them? Body bags are sent to the relatives if they are lucky, preceded by a telegram and some money.

There is colossal loss of human life on all sides and Clinton was mystified why this does not alter any strands of politics or a policy on Kashmir. The massacre in Pahalgam of hundred of innocent pilgrims and labourers (2000) was a horrifying tragedy. Hyper-real media were animated and cashed in. The Prime Minister of India touring the area said that he will not be deterred by the event. Hizbul Majahidin (HM), a militant group, called truce and a dialogue was held. They were told that the talks would make progress only if held within the confines of Indian constitution and sovereignty over Kashmir. In the event, HM withdrew from talks. India's unilateral cease-fire during Ramadan (2000) was a welcome sign, but there was no mention of peace initiatives.

The stereotyped direction in which the events are driven in my view are leading the actors in the conflict into an abyss, too deep and too perilous to cross. It follows therefore that In drawing up a path for progress, our efforts have to reside in philosophical pragmatism, respecting the sensitivities of all parties and using descriptive form of political traditions inclusive of a holistic approach. It may be normative values like prestige and valour need to be undermined. The pageantry of a sword glittering to flaunt nuclear test explosions was euphemistically locking horns. In his vision 2020 for India, the principle scientific advisor stated that " The strategic sectors, fortunately witnessed the growth in nuclear technology "(Kalam) Politicians take notice of the rhetoric, especially coming from authority, loose control and spew polemics. The lex talionis (Eye for Eye) explosions drama became a show piece antic event as if to celebrate a towering victory for the good of the nation.

Epilogue:

I was in conversation with a senior well known Pakistani diplomat and summed up the courage to ask him, why it was that Pakistan does not put the first step forward and pull out forces from Azad Kashmir? It would then, I went on in my rambling, not only make Azad Kashmir government responsible to liberate the other half of Kashmir using diplomatic avenues and pressure tactics, more acceptable to international community, but also identify Pakistan's role in Kashmir as a legitimate help to local freedom struggle. Having recognised Azad Kashmir as an independent country, Pakistan would take the focus from the Indian propaganda away from themselves in international political relations. In theory, Pakistan would support the case for membership of Kashmir in United Nations, so as to enable sovereign Kashmir to seek remedy under the conventions of its charter'. You did guess? The short and brusque reply I received was something like : " Even before we contemplate pulling out from Azad Kashmir, a mere hint would be enough for India to swoop in with its forces and take what is left of Kashmir in freedom". It was a statement and not a point in discourse so I was left to brood over the intensity of the 'fear' and 'mistrust' which pervades the bilateral relations of the two neighbours. There is a 'self fulfilling prophesy' at work when the parties confront each other. One assumes the other party belligerent, engages in hostile action, thereby provoking the other into hostile behaviour, which in turns confirms the original assumption. This is an unending process which will go on for aeons, if not controlled.

As one Indian political analyst put it, "Kashmir is the crown of India". He was looking at a map ! In the same way as K letter in Pakistan is claimed to represent Kashmir. It is these emotions which need to be directed to mutual benevolence from all parties.

The deontological perspective highlights the loss of the benefits in real terms, if Kashmir remains in crisis. Existing doctrines adopted in the name of preserving sovereignty cause invidious misery on innocent people. It is unfortunate that countries, signatories to Human Rights Conventions, predicate laudably the prime concern for their people, still adopt bellicist attitudes resulting in gratuitous violence against the very people that they are trying to rule.

Kashmiris feel stifled with fortifications of lines of control (LOC). They have registered a protest before the international community. "How long do we have to live incarcerated? Time and space both elude us, while days of misery never seem to end, there appears to be no sight of a dawn after a night of waiting". Attempt to subvert dissent correlates in direct proportion with further rise in hardened realism and a separatist doctrine. It is with that background in mind that reconciliatory common theme in all alternatives has been suggested in order to make a new beginning. Peace based on predicated democratic norms may be needed if people are the pivotal factor in a settlement. Time is of essence and we feel the eyes of the world are focused on the events unfolding in the subcontinent. Demilitarisation seems an insurmountable obstacle, I believe because it is taken as a caveat in a settlement. That is why the options considered here make military withdrawal, secondary to the gist of solutions offered. The emphasis is on exigency of taking expeditious steps to stop killings. The hope is to break the mindset stalemate from the present position. Fifty years of deliberations resulted in recalcitrance and hardened attitudes.

We need to put up the 'Christmas tree'. Decorations and fairy lights can be added in all appropriate places. The fairy lights would be the positive signals from all parties and an end to killings. India believes in wearing down insurgency and in time craft its relationship with Srinager on its own terms. Pakistan thinks that time is on their side. Keeping Indian troops occupied weaken India beyond repair. Cognisant of world's inattention, Kashmiris believe time has passed them by. These are blinkers and failed fairy lights which need to be replaced. Celebrating

Peace like the Christmas tree has an intrinsic appeal in any society.

Questions arise when the devolution of power, liberalisation and de-militerisation become centre-region in negotiations. The important first steps must be to recognise legitimacy of the thematic chapters of ethnicity, history, role of relationship with India and Pakistan. It is possible to construct a model of a paradigm on paper.

The players will sit round the table and insert highlights most important to their political interests. The plans may need to be redrawn many times over in order to create new politics faced with a challenging task of balancing theoretical analysis and empirical tests in order to obtain tangible results. We should hopefully have provided enough material for the players to make selections from and maintain the honour and saliency of their national identity in the implementation of the peace process.

Judging from the outcome of agreements reached in the United Nations, Tashkent, Simla, Delhi and Lahore Accord it is likely that a set of powerful catalysts would have to be used in all three phases of the peace process. Bringing parties together, negotiations to arrive at a consensus and signing a treaty and follow through the third phase of implementation of the agreement. Peace committee, would organise the mechanics of this process. We know India has refused mediation, and we also know in bilateral talks, the parties engage in discursive arguments and yet one more meeting is aborted without results. The Peace committee suggested will not be intrusive and have foreign elements which may invite criticism. Help from world community in the form of economic aid, strategic security assistance such as along northern borders and help with modernisation would accelerate the peace effort. I believe we have to execute a stage one of a selected paradigm before even a system of justice, democracy and political development becomes a reality and that elections on a party based liberalist political system is possible.

What Next

In a postscript exercise we have been indulgent in levelling a plan of action which could be initiated as a flow chart or modified with mutual deliberations. Organisation for South Asian Peace (OSAP) of which I am a constituent have been engaged in discussions with academics and politicians and an outline of consensus surfaced which forms the essence of the brief given below, in a sequential order:

1. Seek out representative individuals from each party in conflict, those endowed with a high standard of intellectual attributes and those with neo-liberal views on peace. Individuals who will promote normative ethical values in preference to nationalistic and ethnic atavistic traditions and political pressures influencing their judgement. There are therefore tacit assumptions of who would be entitled to partake in the peace committee. The composition of all cadres of workers would be indigenous, derived from academics and politicians working for peace.

2. Establishment of the Peace Committee office in Nepal or Bangladesh with secretarial facility. The members will work full time and have regular rapport with their respective governments. The office will need to be well organised and adequately funded.

The peace Committee for Kashmir headed by Mr. Ram Jethmalani has made significant progress and could Provide the basic infrastructure and invite representatives from other parties in the dispute.

3. Work would commence to crystallise all modalities of the conflict resolution, using all the professional help already available in the discipline of peace making and group dynamics. Guidance will be sought in problem solving approaches from the treatise available from experts like Edward Azar, Adam Curle, Burton Kelman and others in the field. A fact finding team touring the region would bring a feedback from their research on empirical and factual evidence.

4.   The secretariat gate-keepers will prepare and process the text for the most feasible paradigm which comes the closest to the aspiration of all parties and publish it. Wide dissemination of such a document will bring the issue in pro-active public domain.

In the process of preparing these reports emphasis will be placed upon overriding the preoccupations of the extremist forces and extolling every avenue for signals of peace.

5.   It will be important to streamline the remit of the Peace Committee. A tacit approval from the disputants is not expected in its initial phases. Hard work will be carried out in moderating and reshaping its elements. Brick by brick the building of a framework for the peace process will need to be carried out, methodically and scientifically.

6.   International and local peace organisations will be co-opted and given an active role to play. It may be that religious institutions and world leaders are approached to give their approval and make a contribution. Those verdicts would then be publicised. World leaders can be approached to make a contribution in terms of supporting the peace movement. In the working practices of the peace process it may be useful to prioritise the objectives

7.   A comprehensive package will be prepared and offered to the parties to consider and act upon. The final product would have input from all participants in the peace process.

Promote	Eliminate
Saving lives, restoring confidence in parties	Hostile imagery, dys-information, propaganda
Restoration of amity	Salesmen of arms and defence equipment
Communication at all levels	Vested interests, war mongers, enemies of peace
Propagation of development in peace process	Religious, class ridden and cult fanaticism

Prioritising Fragments of Peace Process

The challenges are formidable and the task to achieve agreements will be difficult. Informed consent from the majority, in the knowledge that a fourth of the world's population with HDI well below 0.3 is at the grassroots of the political system, will require help from multiple sources in the subcontinent. Civil society across the board will need to be educated about the spin off benefits and implications of peace in Kashmir to their own lives. Should we ignore wake up calls like 'Kargil' or the aftermath of the attack on the Indian parliament? These incidents were not an all out war, even so, the withdrawal of western residents alone devastated economy across South Asia.

The argument resides in the challenge of options available to the region. All parties will have to accept the good with the bad. and A balance needs to be struck to bring about a normative way forward for a realistic ending. Safeguards will need to be in place to tone down the interference from hard boiled realists, who may even have support from militarised institutions. One has to bear in mind that there are vested interests inside and outside the disputed region who will always find methods to waylay the peace process. Conflicts can also become a lifestyle for many players in the political world. An open forum strategy is therefore put forth as expedient and more suited a route to pursue. As a strand of the prevailing egocentricism in politics the elite will hold sway in public so that if negotiations are open and informed debate publicised, their followers will continue to eulogise them and keep them in power. Whatever final solution comes about, inevitably the sacrifice would come from the people.

In working out the mechanics of any paradigm, the groundwork would have to start with simultaneous withdrawl of non-Kashmiri forces and decommissioning of weapons by the local militants. The outside militants would have to go back to their countries of orgin. The political parties from all sections of the society would then regroup and start a mandate orientated political lobbying within the framework of the formula agreed upon by all the parties.

The wide spectrum of paradigms described provide a basis for holistic thinking, conflating ideas side by side as prelude to the next stage of psychomas development. In paraphrasing the gist of this work, our own appraisement of this campaign and contemporaneous consensus on the viability of any one paradigm would be listed, in order of merit as Modified Dixon Plan and Partial Autonomy in divided Kashmir. They would stand a chance to be accepted. The utopian vision of Independence is biased in favour of people of Kashmir and excludes interests of India and Pakistan, both of who have heavy stake in the region. The progressive political ideologies will have to prevail and one day make an appreciable impact in the peace process for Kashmir. Ending with a bright note however, there is evidence that increasingly the epistemic communities in the subcontinent recognise the futility of archaic methods of military operations used in what is construed basically a civilian conflict and deploying more forces or reshuffling more military as a strategy, is deemed to be a vacuous panacea for all the challenges. This theory is a corollary of the myth that 'power buys peace'.

Appendix 1

Common Minimal Program Government of Jammu & Kashmir

The coalition government in Jammu & Kashmir comprising of the Congress and People's Democratic Party PDP in coalition with Independent candidates and the JKNPP made a declaration of Common Minimal Program CMP as a bedrock of their governance and constituted the following terms of reference:

Objectives:-

1. The Goal of the Coalition Government is to heal the physsicla, psychological and emotional wounds inflicted by 14 years of militancy, to restore theule of law in Jammu and Kashmir State, to complete the revival of the political process which was begun by the recently concluded elections, and to request the Government of India to initiate and hold, sincerely and seriously, wide ranging consultations and dialogue, without conditions, with the members of the legislature and other segments of public opinion in all the three regions of the state, to evolve a broad-based consensus on restoration of peace with honour in the state.

2. Ensuring safety of lives and properties, restoring dignity and honour of all persons in the state will be the foremost concern of the Government. The Coalition Government will take all possible measures within its power, to protect all the people in the state of Jammu and Kashmir from violence and militancy, whether originating from within or outside the state, and to encourage those young men from the state who have resorted to militancy to return to their families andthe mainstream, with the belief that they will receive security and justice according to law. At the same time, the state government will fully cooperate with the government of India in combating cross-border militancy originating from Pakistan. Restoring Peace and Normalcy and Curbing Corruption.

3. The government shall review all cases of detainees being held without trial for long periods. It shall release all detainees held on non-specific charges, those not charged with serious crimes and those who have been held on charges that are such that the period they have spent in jail exceeds their possible sentence.

4. The government shall review the operation of all such laws that have been used in the past decade to deprive people of their basic rights to life and liberty for long periods of time, without due legal process. Where the Government deems that some special powers need to be retained, it will ensure, by instituting careful and transparent pre-screening and monitoring procedures that such powers are used spariglyand those entrusted with them are held accountable for any misuse.

5. All case of custodial killings and vilations of Human Rights shall be investigated and persons responsible for them will be identified and punished appropriately.

6. The government shall strengthen the State Human Rights Commission to make it an effective instrument for addressing the grievances of the people of the state.

Relief and Rehabilitation

7. The government shall formulate a comprehensive relief and rehabilitation package for those families affected by militant violence over the past decade. The ex-gratia relief at Rupees one lakh per deceased person in militant violence will be raised to Rs. 2 lakhs. In recruitment to government posts, preference will be given to one member of each family where and innocent member has been killed in the militancy related violence.

8. The government shall implement special schemes to rehabilitate former militants who have forsworn violence and rejoined the mainstream.

9. The government will reach out to the children, widows and parents of the deceased militants and make endeavours to provide education to the militancy-affected orphans.

Kashmiri Pandits

10. The government reaffirms that the return of Kashmiri Pandits to their motherland is an essential ingredient of kashmiriat. The government will seek the cooperation of all elements in the society to create and atmosphere conducive to their safe return, will take all necessary steps to ensure their safety and devise effective measures for their rehabilitation and employment.

Jammu Migrants

11. The government will approach the government of India for providing adequate financial assistance for the relief and rehabilitation of the migrants from various disturbed areas of Jammu and Ladakh as well.

Displaced Persons

12. Persons living close to the line of control and the international border face special difficulties due to recurrent tension and cross border violence. Permanent shelters will be constructed in all vulnerable areas to prevent loss of life. The government will also devise a scheme to provide, wherever feasible, alternative land to such families in safe zones.

13. The government shall pursue the matter of due compensation to thoses people from the border areas of Jammu and Kashmir who have suffered loss of crop and cattle due to security operations near LoC and international border.

14. The government shall give top priority to ridding the state adminstration of corruption and nepotism, especially in the award of government jobs and contracts and places in instituitons of higher learning. It will endeavour to make the selection process to all those positons and institutions fully transparent.

Lok Ayukat

15. The government shall establish an institution on 'Ehtisab' for enquiring into complaints received aganist Chief Minister/Ministers and MLAs. The appointment to this post shall be made by the Chief Minister in consultation with the Chief Justice of the State High Court and the Leader of opposition in the Legislative Assembly.

Preparation of an employment orineted medium term development plan laying particular emphasis on the development of agriculture, horticulture, handicrafts, tourism, information technology, food processing and environment friendly industrial activities. Efforts will be made to evolve a development strategy which provides at least one productive job per family.

Employment

Employment and welfare of the young will receive special attention. Measures will be taken to help those youth who have fallen victim to drug abuse and narcotics due to frustration and unemployment.

Committee which deliberated the issues and evolved consensus consisted of Dr. Manmohan Singh, Mr. Arjun Singh, Mr. G. B. Azad, Ms. Ambika Soni (Congress), Mr. Mufti Mohd. Sayeed, Mr. Muzaffar Beig (PDP) and Prof. Bhim Singh (JKNPP).

Source: HTML 1 DocumentEncodingutf-8

Index

1965 War, 125

5th Jt. Convention of Pak-India People's Forum for Peace and Democracy, 51

Abbot, James, 21, 120

Abraham, 32

Accession of Kashmir, 24, 26, 44

Adam Curle, 186

Adams, 114

Afghan Fighters, 116

Afghanistan, 20, 50, 54, 56, 76, 115, 156, 176

Africa, 171

Africa 2000 Forum, 130

African Leaders, 130

Agrarian Development, 136

Airborne Lasers (ABL), 76

Aksai Chin, 38

All Party Huriyat Conference (APHC), 118

Almaty, 130

Al-Queda, 116

Amarnath Cave, 67, 139

America (n), 27, 47, 54, 56, 76, 77, 78, 104, 116, 123, 149, 170, 182

American Politics, 55

American Resolution, 153

American Theatre Missile Defence (TMD), 74, 76

Amman, 80

Amnesty International, 50, 142

Amritsar Treaty, 24, 26

Anarchical System, 23, 47, 118

Anarchy, 141

Angola, 163,164

Angolan War, 162

Ankara and Athens, 149

Anti-America, 136

Anti-Ballistic Missile Treaty, 78

Anti-Imperialist, 24

Anti-Terrorist Coalition, 56

Aparthied Regime, 162

APEC, 130

Arab States, 140

Arc of Islamic Menace, 136

Arc of Noah, 60

Argentina, 79

Aristotle, 139

Arjun Singh, 195

Armed Forces, 100, 154, 157

JK Militia, 154

Kashmir, 154

Pakistan, 154

Armenia and Azers, 26

ASEAN, 130

Asia, 74

Asia Watch, 50

Asian, 41, 104, 131, 143, 150

Asian Military Alliance (AMA), 101, 129, 133-135

Asian Parliament, 113, 129,130, 131, 134-136, 142

Association of Asian Parliamentarian for Peace (AAPP), 50

Athens, 79

Atlantic Ocean, 104

Australia, 171

Australian Journalist, 157

Austrian Throne, 104

Autonomy, 29, 38, 133, 147, 148, 165, 170, 189

'Azad' and Indian Kashmir, 149

'Azad' Kashmir, 42, 170, 183

Azad, GB, 195

Azar, Edward, 23, 186

Balance of Power, 129

Ball, Nicole, 134

Ballistic Missiles, 78, 104

Ballot, 38

Bangalore, 51

Bangalore Declaration, 51

Bangladesh, 50, 132, 186

Bangladesh War, 125

Baramula, 178

BBC, 89

Beas, 20

Beg, Muzaffar, (PDP), 195

Beirut Marines, 76

Belfast Agreement, 166

Belfast Treaty, 147

Benthem, Jeremy, 66

Berlin, 123

Bhim Singh, (JKNPP), 195

Bhutan, 132, 153

Bill Gates Microsoft, 140

Bolshevik, 102

Border Clashes, 77

Border Security Force, 42

Bosnia, 134

Brazil, 78

Britain, 19, 20, 24, 165, 171

British, 6, 18-21, 24, 25-27, 82, 105, 109, 148, 152, 165, 171
　　American Security Information Council, 78
　　and Colorado, 73
　　and Irish, 168
　　Colonial Rule, 153
　　Diplomacy, 27
　　History, 173
　　India, 25
　　Kashmir, 173
　　Legacy, 25
　　Occupation, 39
　　Rule, 26
　　Ruled Kashmir, 173
　　Supremacy, 20

Brussels for Europe, 131

Buddhist, 100, 139, 152

Bunkers, 76

Bush Administration, 41

Cameroon, 171

Camp David, 94, 127, 139, 94

Canadian Nuclear Reactor Technology, 77

Caribbean Sea, 169

Caste System, 134

Caucasus, 56, 116

Ceasefire, 5, 125, 182

Ceasefire Violations, 90

Central America, 168

Central Asia, 20, 50, 54, 105

Chagos Island, 26

Chechnya, 116, 130, 164

Chechnya and Kosovo, 99

Chechnyan Devastation, 99

Chemical Oxygen Laser Weapons, 76

Chemical Weapons, 79

China, 23, 38, 48, 74, 76, 84, 100, 133, 149

China, India and Pakistan, 169

Chinese Kashmiri, 60

Chirac, 133

Chitisingpora and Anantnag, 67

Christian, 32

Christmas, 184

Churchill, 47

CICA, 130

City Square (Lal Chowk), 89

Civil Disobedience, 34

Civil Liberties, 60

Civil War, 62, 100, 126, 62

Civilization of -18, 23, 34

    Central Asia, 23

    Tibetan-Chinese, 23

    South Asia, 23

Clausewitz, Von, 84

Clinton, Bill, 48, 55, 78, 139, 181, 182

Coalition Government, 191, 192

Cold War, 48, 99, 103, 115, 162, 164

Cold War Politics, 18

Collective Security, 129, 134, 135

Colombo, 181

Colonial Vassal State, 173

Colonialism, 49

Colonising Process, 26

Colorado, 109

Commerce, 106

Common Minimum Programme, (CMP), 7, 191

Commonwealth Nations, 26

Communication, 49, 103, 104, 138, 150, 153, 154, 155, 167, 176

    System, 76, 109

Communism, 53, 80

Communist Forces, 163

Constituent Assembly, 61

Conventional Weapons, 40, 41

Conventions on Disarmament, 74

Costa Rica, 168, 169

CPM, 7

CR Drug Traffickers, 169

CR Hydroelectric Power, 169

Cross-Border Militancy, 192

Cruce, Emric, 102, 106

Cuba and Berlin, 48

Cuba, 163, 164

Cultural and Trade Relations, 159

Cultural Exchanges, 155

Culture of Violence, 102

Curzon, Lord, 26

Custodial Killings, 80

Customs and Excise, 165

Cyprus, 149, 170

Dalai Lama, 100

Dar-es-Salem, 76

Darwinian Evolution, 108

Decolonisation, 99, 131, 134

Defence, 73, 102, 138, 150, 154, 155, 166

Defence and Collective Security, 132

Defence Budget of Pakistan, 40

Defence Communication, 38

Defence Industry, 56

Delhi, 89, 185

Demilitarization, 47, 167, 172, 184, 185

Derrida, Jaques (French), 56, 99

Despotism, 29, 152

Dhaka Declaration, 74

Diamond Mines, 162

Dichotomy, 141

Dilip Singh, 20

Dilli, 47, 116

Directed Energy Weapons, 76

Dixit, JN, 152

Dixon Plan, 156, 158, 159

Dixon Sir Owen, 45, 156, 157

Doda, 178

Dogra Regimes, 173

Dogra Rule, 25

Downing Street Declaration, 168

Dublin and London, 166

Earthquake Bombs, 76

East Asia, 41, 133

East India Company, 20, 26

East Jerusalem, 139

East Timor, 38, 47, 99, 116, 124, 164, 171

East Timories, 99

Eastern Europe, 54, 55, 130

Eastern European States, 173

Economic

    Cooperative, 97

    Development, 40

    Growth, 102, 176

    Integration, 137

    Race, 102

    Relations, 102

    System, 102

Economy, 59, 135, 136, 138, 150, 154, 155, 178

Economy of Kashmir, 152

Economy, Cooperation, 141

Education, 176, 138, 140

Egypt, 78

Eid, 7

El Salvador, 169

Election (s), 38, 47, 56, 61, 116, 127, 136, 143, 162, 164, 166

Elections Electoral System, 165

Electro-magnetic Pulse Warheads, 76

England, 165

Environmental and Health Issues, 106

Ethics, 154

Ethnic Divide, 17

Ethnic Riots, 24

Ethno-Centricism, 159

Ethnological, 23

Europe, 76, 108, 137, 140, 141

European, 131, 151

European Army, 133

European China, 170

European Community, 158

European Human Right Law, 66

European Union, 132, 165

Evans, Michael (Defence Journalist), 73

Fascism, 53

Fascist, 140

Fascist Institution, 131

Federal System, 137

Federalist Quadrangular Relationship, 150

Feudalist Dynasties, 143

Fiji, 26, 49

Finite Time Singularity, 90

Fishlock, Trevor, 89

Foreign Affairs, 38

Forsythe, David, 85

Foucalt, Michael, 86

France, 17, 40, 74, 76, 139, 141, 165, 171

Free Ball Bomb, 78

Free Economy, 29

Free Market, 105

Free Trade, 102, 106

Freedom Fighters, 164

Freedom House, 50

Freedom Struggle, 99, 183

French, 170

French Revolution, 33, 35, 79

Fukuyama, Francis, 38, 53, 108

Fundamentalism, 54, 56, 82, 99

Gandhi, Indira, 49, 126

Gandhi, M.K., 24, 33-35, 91

Gandhian Philosophy, 33

GDP, 41

General Assembly Resolution, 67

Genocide of Jews, 66

Geo-Political Lines, 23

Georgia, 42

German Army, 82

German, 57, 83

Germans and Spanish, 170

Germans, 79, 162, 163, 171

Germany, 40, 79, 131, 162, 164

Ghali, Boutros, 5, 133

Ghaza. 123, 124, 126

Gilgiat-Baltistan People Forum, 148

Gilgiat-Baltistan, 148

Glancy Commission, 19

Global Anarchy, 49

Globalization, 104, 105, 107, 137, 140, 153, 164

Great Britain, 27, 66, 77, 165

Greeks and Turks, 149

Green Art of Jihad, 56

Green Islamic Menace, 99

Green Revolution, 178

Gregory IX (Pope), 89

Grotius, Hugo, 5

Guatemala, 79, 169

Gulab Singh (Maharaja), 19, 20, 21, 25, 157

Gulbadin or Usama-bin-Ladin, 77

Gulf War, 104

Gurdaspur and Zira Dist., 21

Guyana, 26

Hallbrook, Richard, 47

Hampson, 44

Handicraft Exports, 153

Handicrafts, 194

Harding, Sir Henry, GG, 20

Hardy, Justice, 79

Hebrew, 31

Hegal, George, 57

Hegal, GWF, 83

Hegal's Teaching, 109

Helsinki Final Act, 135

Himachal, 120

Himalayan, 59, 87, 90, 105, 106, 124

    Fox, 19

    Paradise, 20

    States. 153

Himalayas and Pamirs, 169

Hindu, 47, 108, 152

    and Muslim Fundamentalist, 85

    and Muslims, 156, 175

    Extremist, 33

    India, 56

    Pilgrimage, 67, 139

    Scriptures, 32

Hindus, 118, 135, 139

Hindus of Kashmir, 42

Hird, Douglas, 54

Hiroshima, 89

Hisbolah, 54, 56

Hitler, 79

Hizbul Mujahidin (HM), 39, 80, 118, 182

Ho Chi Minh, 170

Hobbeman, 138, 141

Holy Shrine, 140

Home Affairs, 138

Homer, 105

Honduras, 169

Hong Kong, British, 150

Human Development Index (HDI), 41, 188

Human Rights, 27, 29, 48, 50, 66, 116, 135, 177, 181

    Commissions, 192

    Convention, 184

    Violation, 50

    Abuses, 29, 40

Hume, 120

Huriyat, 77, 163

Hyper Real Media, 142, 144, 182

Idgah, 105

IFAD, 178

Illegal Occupation (Kashmir), 43

Illiteracy, 178

Ilwa Community, 26

IMF, 116, 176, 178

Imperialism, 54

Independence of India Act, 154

India (n), 17, 19, 20, 21, 23, 24, 25, 26, 29, 30, 35, 37, 38, 39, 40, 41, 43, 44, 47, 48, 51, 54, 55, 56, 59, 73, 75, 77, 78, 78, 81,

84, 87, 88, 86, 90, 94, 98, 100, 102, 107, 109, 113-115, 118, 119, 125,127, 131, 135, 140, 141, 143-145, 152, 154, 155-157, 161, 162, 179, 181, 183-185, 189, 192, 193

India and Pakistan, 5, 6, 24, 27, 30, 32, 33, 37, 38-40, 41, 44, 47, 48, 49, 50, 51, 56, 60, 73, 74-76, 77, 78, 84, 85, 87, 88, 89, 97, 100, 102-104, 105, 107, 116, 117, 124, 125, 126, 129, 132, 133, 136-140, 142, 143, 145, 148-150, 153-155, 155, 156, 158, 162, 163-167, 171-173, 176, 178, 185, 189

India, Pakistan and Kashmir, 102

India, Weapons, 77

Indian

    Airlines, 86, 89

    and Pakistani Currencies, 143

    and Pakistani Military, 100

    Armed Forces, 53

    Army, 23, 86, 89, 154

    Constitution, 38, 39, 47, 126, 182

    Freedom Fighters, 109

    Independence Act, 26

    Kashmir, 60, 150, 168, 170

    Leaders, 38

    Media, 61

    Parliament, 188

    PM, 126, 182

    President Awards, 153

    Propaganda, 183

    Security Forces, 54

    Troops, 184

Indo Pakistan, 48

    peace, 133

    war, 44, 49

Indonesia, 99, 124, 170, 171

Indonesian in East Timor, 162

Indonesian Troops, 171

Industrial Growth, 106

Industry, 140, 144, 176, 178

Industry, Export Oriented, 102

Information Technology, 194

Instrument of Charter, 152

Insurgency, 25, 85, 87, 184

Insurgent Group, 53

Insurgents, 17, 77, 103

International

    Border (s), 113, 123-125, 194

    Capitalism, 107

    Conventions, 153

    Court of Justice, 44, 163

    Covenant on Civil and Political Rights, 153

    Extremist Movement, 99

    Human Rights, 50

    Law(s), 66, 100, 140

    Politics, 124

    Relations, 26, 130, 138, 152, 154, 163

    Security, 75, 99

IRA, 80, 166

Iran, 54

Iran and North Korea, 78

Iraq, 104

Iraq and Libya, 78

Ireland, 78

Irish and English, 167

Islam, 32, 56

Islamabad, 166

Islamic, 77, 99

    Cultural Identity, 99

    Extremist, 54

    Fundamentalism, 56, 58

    Fundamentalist, 80

    Green Menace, 54

    Menace, 56

    Rule, 53

    Solidarity, 50

    World, 56

Israel, 78, 80, 114, 124

Israel and Palestine, 139

Israeli, 94

Istanbul, 130

IT Industrial Bases, 107

Italian Society, 142

Jakarta, 116

Jalaludin Rumi, 71

Jammu, 19, 23, 148, 193

Jammu and Anantnag (Kashmir), 51

Jammu and Kashmir, 7, 18, 19, 20, 42, 47, 51, 91, 143, 148, 155, 157, 191, 192,

Jammu and Ladakh, 156

Jammu Kashmir Liberation Front (JKLF), 39, 53, 77, 151, 155

Jammu Migrants, 193

Japan and Germany, 75

Japanese, 123, 170

Jaswant Singh, 81

Jefferson, Thomas, 153

Jerusalem, 66, 94, 126, 139

Jesus Christ, 32

Jewish and Arab Diaspora, 32

JKNPP, 191

JKPDM, 77

Judicial System, 81, 176

Judiciary, 136, 138, 166, 169

Jung, Carl, Swiss Psy., 30

Kant, E, 179

Kantian, 55

Karachi, 103, 155

Kargil, 77, 188

Kargil Episode, 49, 73

Kargil War, 48, 86, 87, 119

Karl Marx, 108

Kashmir, 5-7, 17-19, 20, 21, 23, 24, 25, 26, 27, 29, 31, 32, 33-35, 37, 38-44, 47, 48, 50, 51, 53-61, 65-67, 69, 71, 73-91, 93, 94, 97-111, 113-121, 123-127, 129, 131, 132, 134, 135, 136-140, 137, 141-145, 147, 148, 150-153, 154, 155-157, 159, 161-167, 168-170, 171, 172, 173, 175, 175-179, 181-184, 186, 187, 198, 194

    Accord, 126

    Assembly, 29

    Conflict, 53, 120, 166

    Constituency, 30

    Dispute, 7, 17, 29, 57, 73, 79, 81, 84, 98, 99, 101, 125, 131, 133, 142, 163, 168, 171

    Dissident Parties, 38

    East, 149

    Huriyat Conference, 155

Economic and Social Charac
teristics in-, 176
Life Expectancy, 41
Peace Building in-, 177
Peace Wheel for -, 180
Political Status, 173
Socio-economic Progress, 175
Violent Conflict Region, 41
West, 149
Women of-, 88
Kashmiri (s), 21, 23, 26, 33, 42, 59,
62, 77, 87, 88, 108, 118, 136,
155, 158, 184
Civilian, 181
Diaspora, 175
Group, 77
Leaders, 50
Militants, 89
Origin, 148
Pandits, 193
Kashmiriat, 193
Kashmiris Craftsmen, 107
Kelman, Burton, 186
Khyber Pass, 20
King, Martin Luther, 91, 117
Kissinger, 54
Kofi Annan, 47, 116
Korea, 149
Kosovo or Palestine, 99
Kosovo, 53, 99
Kosygin, Alexia (PM), 49
Kropotkin's, 7
Kullu Valley, 20
Kupwara, 69, 178
Kurd, 79
Kuwait, 104, 124

Ladakh, 148, 193
Ladakh and Jammu, 82, 151
Lahore, 115, 180
Accord, 185
Declaration, 126, 180
Laughan, Sean, Journalist, 89
League of Nations, 171, 172
Lebanon, 54
Lenin, 102
Lethal Weapons, 73
Liberalism, 38, 53
Liberalist, 142, 182
Liberalist Political System, 185
Line of Control (LoC), 26, 84, 106,
113, 117, 123-125, 184, 194
Literacy, 41
Locke, John, 141
Lok Ayukt, 194
Low Intensity Perpetual War (LIPEW),
40

Machiavellian Policies, 26
MacMahon Line, 38
Macro-Economic, 143, 150
Mafia Gangs, 80
Mahayana Buddhism, 32
Mandi, 20
Manmohan Singh, 195
Mao Tse-Tung, 39
Marx, Karl, 31, 88
Marxist Theory, 135
Masservy, Sir Frank, 24
Mauritius, 26
Mazzini, Giuseppe (Italian)
Mc Naughton, AGL, 44
McDonald, Tom, 78

Mckenan, Don, 49

Mecca, 139

Mediterranean Island, 170

Mexican, 124

Mexico, 78

Micro-Economy, 143

Middle East, 77

Migration, 26, 42, 62

Militancy, 30, 177, 178, 191, 192

Militant Group, 39, 54, 182

Militant Insurgent, 77

Militant Nationalism, 137

Militant Organization, 51, 132

Militants, 39, 54, 71, 77, 80, 81, 82, 86, 89, 106, 144, 189

    Kashmir, 39

Militarism, 63, 67

Military Alliance, (AMA), 113

Military Engineers, 29

Military Operation in Kashmir, 24

Missile Defence Capability, 76

Missiles, 41

Missile Deployment, 75

Modified Dixon Plan, 113, 150, 157, 159, 189

Mongolia, 105

Montaigue, Michael de, 114

Montevldeo Convention, 138

Moro Nationalist, 50

Morocco and Mauritania, 170

Mountbatten, 21, 24, 154

Mughabe, Robert, 130

Mujahidin, 56

Multilaterism, 165

Multi-track Diplomacy, 119

Muslim (s), 20, 23, 42, 55, 56, 79, 100, 139, 152, 158

Muslim Population, 152

Muslim Refugee, 118

Muslim State, 142

Mussolini, 142

Muttahida Majlis-e-Amal, 136

Muzafarabad, 156, 158

Mysore, 140

Naik, Niaz A, 180

Nairobi, 76

Namibia, 38, 161-164, 171, 172

Namrana Group, (Niaz Mallik), 119

Narayan, Jayaprakash, 39, 81

Natanyahu, Benjamin, 80

National Conference Party, 124

National Conference, 7, 63, 77

Nationalism, 38, 55, 84, 137

Nationalist, 6

    Forces, 51

    Movement, 80

NATO, 54, 55, 73, 99, 116, 133, 152

NATO's Security Strategy, 5

Nawaz Sherif, 126

Nehru, Jawaharlal (Indian PM), 23, 24

Neo-Marxist Social Democracy, 156

Nepal, 86, 132, 152, 153, 186

Neutral States, 78

New Agenda Coalition (NAC), 78

New Delhi, 38, 87, 166

New Nuclear States, 78

New World Order, 54

New York, 62, 74, 164

New Zealand, 78

NGO, 50, 104, 109, 132, 137, 176

Nicaragua and Panama, 169

Nimitz, Chester W (F.A), 44

Non-Kashmiri Armies, 163

Non-Kashmiri Forces, 189

Non-Proliferation Treaty, 74, 78

Non-Violence, 34

North and South Cyprus, 149, 170

North and South Korea, 123

North and South Vietnam, 170

North East India, 102

North Korea, 150

North South Divide, 117

North Western Region, 23

Northern Borders, 185

Northern Ireland, 26

Northern Island, 77, 166-168

Norway, 104

No-War Pact, 126

Nuclear, 77, 135

    and Missile Warfare, 130

    Arms, 73, 74

    Arsenal, 74, 101

    Base, 26

    Capabilities, 73

    Disarmament, 77

    Exchange, 74

    Explosion, 117

    Power, 75, 76, 101

    Strike, 73

    Technology, 182

    Test Explosion, 182

    Threats, 58

    War, 73, 78, 104, 78

    Weapon Table, 74

    Weapons, 74, 99

Nuclearisation, 74

Oligarchic Rule, 61

Oliver and Richard Cromwell, 173

Organisation for Security and Coop. In Europe (OSCE), 129, 130, 134, 135

Organization for South Asian Peace, (OSAP), 50, 186

Organization of Islamic Countries (OIC), 50

Osama-bin-Laden, 116

Oslo Track II Mediation, 114

Ottoman Empire, 171

Pacific Ocean, 169

Pacifism, 33

Pahalgam, 182

Pakistan, 6, 23, 29, 35, 38, 42-44, 47, 51, 54-56, 77, 78, 84, 86, 88, 90, 94, 98, 102, 107, 109, 115, 118, 120, 125, 127, 129, 135, 136, 140, 144, 145, 149, 150, 155, 156, 158, 161, 163,165, 170, 179, 180, 183, 184, 192

Pakistan and China, 130

Pakistan and India, 22

Pakistan Army, 23, 73, 77

Pakistan Nuclear Facility, 75

Pakistan, Military Regime, 49

Pakistan's Rule, 168

Pakistani Kashmir, 60

Pakistani Militants, 37

Palestine, 26, 53, 80, 108, 126, 127, 155, 171

Pamir Range, 105

Panjab, 19, 103, 120

Panun Kashmir, 148

Parliamentary, 39

Partisans of Ukraine, 82

Partition Process, 25

Partition, 25, 87, 152, 157, 170

Pathans, 23

Patition, 17, 24

Pattan (Kashmir), 61

PDP, 191

Peace Agencies, 54

Peace and Security, 44

Peace Committee, (1953), 24, 185-187

Peace Initiatives, 182

Peace Making, 31, 32

Peace Settlement, 178

Peace Treaty, 20

Peace Wheel, 87

People Democratic Party, 77

People's Democratic Party, (PDP), 7

Phillippines, 50

Plato, 104, 129

Plebiscite, 38, 43-45, 89, 100, 114, 154, 156-158, 162-164, 171, 179

PLO, 80, 114

Pluralism, 150, 156

Policy of Irredentism, 37

Political Culture, 106

Political Freedom, 177

Political Migration, 134

Political Party, 38

Political System, 169, 188

Poll Pott (Cambodia), 79

Poonch, 148

Populist Menace, 153

Portuguese, 99

Post Cold War, 44

Post Colonial Period, 23

Post World War Era, 172

POTA (Prevention of Terrorist Act), 7

Preferred Nation Status, 48

Princely States, 25, 152

Prisoners of War, 125

Production Economy, 89

Protracted Social Conflict, (PC), 23

Punjab, 19, 103, 120

Putin, 78

Putin, Valadimir Russian President, 76

Qaziabad, 69

Qunel Village, 69

Quran, 32

Radcliffe, Cyril, 21, 120

Radical Humanism, 141

Raj Days, 69

Ramadan, 182

Rani Jindan, 19

Raphael, 48

Rascal of Asia, 20

Red Russian Revanchism, 99

Regional Security, 133

Rome, 139

Roosevelt, 47

Rouge Nations, 78

Rousseau, Jean Jacques, 33, 110

Roy, Manabendra, 141

Rubsenstein, 80

Russia, 26, 40, 74, 76, 104, 105, 115, 116, 130

    and China, 54

Russian (s), 104, 114, 164

Russian Army, 82

Russian Invasion, 123

Rwanda, 53

SAARC, 130

SAARC Summit, 181

Saddam Hussain, 79, 104, 124

SAFTA, 130

Sahrawis, 170

Saichan Heights, 90

Sarajevo, 104

Satellite Imaging Data, 73

Satyagaha, 34

Saudi Arabia, 41

Saudi Khobar Towers, 76

Sayeed, Mufti Mohd., 195

Schruder, 131

Science and Technology, 75

Sector,

    Agriculture and Forest, 153

    Handicraft, 178

    Mechanised, 178

    Power Generation, 178

    Technical, 135

Security Council Resolutions, 164

Security, 23, 40, 41, 48, 54, 77, 93, 99, 100, 119, 129, 133, 135, 138, 145, 148, 149, 150, 155, 162, 166, 178, 185, 192, 194

Security Council, 44, 115, 44

Security Environment, 74

Security Forces, 40, 155

Security Policy, 77

Self-Determination, 55, 56, 99, 113, 116, 152, 153, 154, 163, 165

Separatist Doctrine, 184

Serbian, 99

Shared Pooled Sovereignty, 129

Sharman (Gen), 42

Shastri, Lal Bahadur (PM), 49, 126

Sheikh Imam, 21

Sheikh Abdullah, 24, 126

Siachin Heights, 90

Shiv Sena, 158

Sikh Army, 19

Sikh Rulers, 19

Sikh War II, 20

Sikhs, 19, 20, 21, 42

Sikkim, 153

Silicon Valley, 141

Silk Road, 38

Simla, 113, 185

Simla Accord, 47

Simla Agreement, 125

Social and Economic Development Programme, 177

Social Contract, 24, 32, 67

Social Justice, 59, 130, 141

Social Order, 33

Social Welfare, 40

Socialisation, 140

Societal Corporatism, 142

Society (ies), 6, 18, 23, 25, 33, 39, 44, 54, 59-63, 67, 71, 82, 85, 86, 101, 107, 118, 136, 142, 151, 157, 185, 193

    Civil, 115, 119, 145, 159, 172, 176, 177, 178, 188, 189

    Epistemic, 6

    Functional, 140

    India, 33

    Multi-Ethnic, 154, 159

Socrates, 32, 79

Soni, Ambika, 195

Sophia Antepolis, 141

Sopore, 178

Soros Foundation, 50

South Africa, 78, 162-163, 171

South African (s), 130, 162

South African Army, 163

South African Society, 104

South African Whites, 162

South Asia, 23, 41, 55, 74, 77, 116, 129, 130, 132-134, 181, 188

South Asian, 100, 137

South Asian Community, 129, 133

South Asian Nations, 130

South Asian Partition, 113

South Asian Politics, 53, 56

South Kashmir, 148

Southern Island, 77

Soviet Military, 173

Soviet Union, 49, 173

Soviets, 48

Sri Lanka, 53, 132

Srinagar, 131, 184

    Sectt., 132

St.Augustine, 32

St.Thomas Aquinas, 32

Stalin, 26, 79

Star War Technology, 76

State Task Force, 7

Stinger Missiles, 116

Submarines, 104

Sunderji, SK, 75

Super Wars, 104

Supreme Court, 158

Sutlej and Kashmir Border, 20

SWAPO in Namibia, 39, 163

Sweden, 78

Switz Style Cantons, 134

Syria, 171

Tanganyika, 171

Tashkent (Russian City), 49, 185

Tashkent Agreement, 125

Task Force, 82

Technology Park, 110

Terrorism, 49, 54, 58, 73, 79, 80, 81, 130

    and Fundamentalism, 50

Terrorist, 77, 79, 80, 81, 82

    Group, 103

Thabo Mbeki, 130

The Times, London, 73

Tiananmin Square, 48

Tibet, 20, 23, 105, 153

Tibetan Border, 38

Tibetan Economy, 100

Togoland, 171, 172

Tomahawk Missiles, 76

Totalitarianism, 173

Tourism, 97, 102, 143, 152, 169, 194

Tourist Industry, 136

Trade, 105, 148, 149, 150

Trade and Commerce, 135

Trade and Supplies, 20

Trade and Tourism, 105

Trans Jordan and Iraq, 171

Treaty of Amritsar, 20

Treaty of Westphalia, 5

Tribal Invaders, 24

Trusteeship Council, 172

Truth Commissions and Tribunals, 177

Turkish and Greek, 149

Twang Tract (Tibet), 38

UDHR, 85

     Article, (21), 39

UK, 40, 50, 56, 74

UN, 157, 162-164, 171, 172, 179, 183, 185

     Charter, 140, 153

     Commission for India & Pakistan (UNCIP), 43, 44

     Development Programme, (UNDP), 176, 178

     Foundational Doctrine, 152

     General Assembly Resolution, 100

     Intervention, 25

     Observers, 116

     Resolutions, 44, 47, 116

     Role in Namibia, 161

     Secretary General Kofi Annan 170

     Security Council 115

UNCIP, 115, 156, 162

Underground Warfare, 82

UNICEF, 178

UNICP, 47

Unionist, 168

Unionist Paramilitary Groups, 166

UNITA, 163

United Asia, 100

United Kashmir, 148

United Nations, 43, 44, 66, 90, 106, 113, 115, 116, 117, 133, 141, 149, 152, 153

United Nations Human Right Commission, (UNHRC), 50

United Nations Resolutions, 5

Universal Declaration on Human Rights, 65

Unmanned Aircraft, 76

Upanishads, 32

Uranium, 78

US Agency for International Development, 176

US and Soviet Nuclear Competition, 48

US Constitution, 60

US Missile Defence System, 41

US Policy on Kashmir, 49

USA, 17, 40, 41, 47-49, 54, 55, 56, 61, 74, 74, 76, 85, 104, 114, 130, 158

     and Russia, 78

USA Security Umbrella, 76

US-Cole Warship in Aden, 76

USSR, 48, 49, 116, 125, 162

Uzbecks and Tajiks, 26

Vajpayee, Indian PM, 6, 115, 126, 131

Vale-Muzafarabad Region, 158

Vatican, 139

Versailles, 5

Veto Power, 163

Victoria, Queen, 20

Vienna Congress, 5

Vietnam, 149, 170

Violence, 25, 27, 30, 33, 35, 39, 40, 41, 42, 47, 48, 50, 51, 53, 55, 57, 59, 71, 80, 81, 86, 90, 99, 102, 106, 123, 137, 142, 157, 167, 168, 176, 181, 182, 192

Violence, Political, 172

Washington, 47, 133

Welfare State, 156

West Bank, 123, 125

Western Countries, 55

Western Hierarchy, 49

Western Powers, 47, 163

Western Sahara, 170

White House, 182

Wilson, Woodrow, 56

Wolf, Virginia, 90

Women Peace Initiative in South Asia, 51

World Bank, 176, 178

World Trade Centre, .76, 107

World Trade Organization, 48

World War I, 104, 171

Xingiang, 54, 56

Yeats, WB (Irish Poet), 63

Zartmam, 88

Zen, 32

Zero Sum Contest, 40

Zimbabwe, 49, 130